INSIGHT COMPACT GUIDES

London

Compact Guide: London is the ultimate easy-reference guide to one of the world's most stimulating cities. It tells you everything you need to know about London's great attractions, from St Paul's Cathedral to Madame Tussaud's, from the British Museum to Harrods.

This is just one title in *Apa Publications'* new series of pocket-sized, easy-to-use guidebooks intended for the independent-minded traveller. Based on an award-winning formula pioneered in Germany, *Compact Guides* pride themselves on being up-to-date and authoritative. They are in essence mini travel encyclopedias, designed to be comprehensive yet portable, both readable and reliable.

D1241854

Star Attractions

An instant reference
to some of London's
most popular tourist
attractions to help
you on your way.

National Gallery p15

*Houses of Parliament
p17*

*Westminster Abbey
p19*

Covent Garden p23

*St Paul's Cathedral
p27*

*The Tower of London
p30*

*The British Museum
p36*

Hyde Park p46

*Piccadilly
Circus p14*

*The Victoria and
Albert Museum p52*

Windsor Castle p64

London

Introduction

Places

Culture

Leisure

Practical Information

London – A City for All Seasons

There can hardly be another city anywhere in the world which is cosmopolitan and yet also a microcosm of the nation of which it is a part. It is said that there is no British town or city which is 'more English' than London. It is an almost perfect reflection of the British way of life and yet a visit to London can be like a world tour. London is home to people from all corners of the world and it is possible to sample something of their lifestyle in their part of London, in their community, and in their cafés and restaurants offering their local food and drink. London unites Britain and the rest of the world.

It has something to offer everyone: interesting old buildings, beautiful parks and gardens, some of the finest museums and monuments in the world, a wide range of sporting and recreational facilities, some of Europe's best theatres, top-class opera houses, one of the biggest zoos in the world, crowded shopping streets, royal palaces, smoky pubs, and reminders of distant oceans amid the once grimy streets and alleys of the old Docklands, which is now undergoing dramatic changes.

It is not correct to talk of a 'London atmosphere', because there is no such thing. Every part of this huge city has its own distinct atmosphere. An understanding of the history of the city can explain this phenomenon: London developed slowly, spreading outwards as numerous small towns and villages merged together. Even today, the 'special atmosphere' in any one of the different areas can often be explained by reference to its historical background.

There is dignified Westminster, for example, with the government buildings of Whitehall and the Houses of Parliament, the colourful West End, a magnet for shoppers and entertainment-seekers, refined Mayfair for the very wealthy, lively and daring Chelsea for the young and artistic, slightly seedy Soho with its night-life and restaurants, the City, the financial heart of the nation, fashionable Kensington with its world-famous museums, aristocratic Belgravia, intellectual Bloomsbury, home to London University and the British Museum, Holborn and its law courts and then the poorer quarters in the East End with its street markets, Jewish Whitechapel and so on. Together they make a city of variety and contrasts. It may not be the world's most beautiful metropolis, but it is certainly one of the most interesting places for tourists and travellers.

Position and size

Londoners with a sense of humour like to say that London lies at the centre of the world and Piccadilly Circus is the world's navel. If you wait there long enough, then every human being on the planet will eventually pass by.

*Opposite:
the sound of London*

Double-decker delights

5

Cycling along the Thames

Hyde Park hiatus

Street-wise Stradivari

On a more matter-of-fact level, London lies just south of Berlin and just north of Vancouver on 51.30N latitude, but of course it also could be said to span both halves of the globe, as the Greenwich Meridian, the point that defines the zero line of longitude, passes through Greenwich at the Old Royal Observatory.

Situated about 40 miles (64km) from the mouth of the Thames, the built-up area of London extends along both banks of the river over gently undulating terrain with elevations of up to 45ft (15m). Calculating the surface area of London is a difficult task. The city covers 115sq miles (300sq km), the historical City of London is only 1 square mile (2.6sq km), whereas the jurisdiction of the Metropolitan Police extends over 700sq miles (1875sq km) which is double the area covered by New York's police.

Climate

To be fair to London, the weather is not as bad as its reputation suggests. There are many days in the year when it does not rain and, contrary to popular belief, except in November and December, there are very few really foggy days. Rain falls on the capital on between 170 and 200 days a year, mainly in late autumn and winter. The annual mean temperature is 9°C with no great variations. In summer, the average temperature is between 16°C and 17°C and in winter between 2°C and 4°C. Generally speaking, long periods of sub-zero temperatures are rare and snow never seems to stay on the ground for very long. The spring weather is cool but not cold and a heavy winter coat should not be necessary. A raincoat, however, is an essential item. In summer the weather is usually fine with long sunny periods and in July and August, temperatures of up to 28°C can be reached. Autumn is normally a pleasant time as the wet weather does not usually arrive until later in the year.

Population and administration

Around 6.8 million people live in Greater London, making it one of the largest cities in the world. The City of London is sometimes referred to as the Square Mile and is, in fact, home to only around 5,000 inhabitants. It is the smallest of the boroughs which make up the metropolitan area and it is administered by the Corporation of London. The City consists of 25 wards and each ward is represented by an alderman. The 25 aldermen, who are elected for life, and 130 Common Council men, meet together in the Common Council. Each year an alderman is chosen to be the Lord Mayor of London.

The Griffin, London's symbol

The other boroughs are: Barking, Barnet, Bexley, Brent, Bromley, Camden, Croydon, Ealing, Enfield, Greenwich, Hackney, Hammersmith and Fulham, Haringey, Harrow, Havering, Hillingdon, Hounslow, Islington, Kensington and Chelsea, Kingston-upon-Thames, Lambeth, Lewisham, Merton, Newham, Redbridge, Richmond-upon-Thames, Southwark, Sutton, Tower Hamlets, Waltham Forest, Wandsworth and Westminster.

7

Until March 1986, the Greater London Council was the administrative body responsible for Greater London, but it was abolished on 1 April 1986, making London the only major city in the world without a unified administration. Its functions were either delegated to the boroughs or taken over by government ministries. The reasons for the abolition of the GLC were primarily political as the socialist-controlled council strenuously opposed the policies of Margaret Thatcher's Conservative government. Many people feel that this lack of central coordination adversely affects the quality of life in the city, especially in areas such as public transport.

Religion

The majority of London's churchgoers belong to the Church of England, which is independent of the crown and of the government, but the Roman Catholic Church's hierarchy is retained. Within the Church of England, three strands can be identified: the High Church, which emphasises ceremony in the Catholic tradition, the Low Church, which is more in line with Protestant traditions of adherence to the scriptures, and the Broad Church, which favours a liberal interpretation of the creed. Catholics, Methodists, Baptists, Presbyterians and Jews also have numerous places of worship in the capital; there are also a number of mosques as well as Sikh and Hindu temples.

A beefeater barks

Guildhall interior

The Guilds

The so-called Guilds or Livery Companies, which are the successors to the medieval religious fraternities, crafts or social guilds, reflect an interesting aspect of London's history. There are 95 Guilds in all, of which 12 make up the Greater Companies. They are the Mercers, Grocers, Drapers, Fishmongers, Goldsmiths, Skinners, Merchant Taylors, Haberdashers, Salters, Ironmongers, Vintners and Clothworkers. These companies play an important role in the administration of the City. Most of their 'halls', of which there are a total of 25, including the Grocers' Hall, Drapers' Hall, Fishmongers' Hall etc, date from the Middle Ages and, although they are not generally open to outsiders, they provide some of London's finest examples of medieval architecture.

Queen Elizabeth I

The Royal Family

The United Kingdom of Great Britain and Northern Ireland is a hereditary, constitutional monarchy, but the Royal Family have no legislative power. This power resides with parliament which has a lower and an upper house – the elected *House of Commons* and the appointed *House of Lords*. In 1837, Buckingham Palace became Queen Victoria's official residence and since then all British monarchs have lived there.

Kensington Palace is the home of Princess Margaret, the Duke and Duchess of Gloucester and Prince and Princess Michael of Kent. The Queen Mother lives in London at Clarence House, where the Duke and Duchess of Kent have an apartment. Prince Charles also stays here when in London.

Houses of Parliament

Historical Highlights

In pre-Roman times, present-day London was the site of a Celtic settlement and it is possible that the name London derives from the Celtic *Llyn-din*, which was later to become *Londinium* during the Roman occupation. For Cunobelius, the Celtic king of southern England (c 5BC–AD40), London was already an important port.

AD43 Roman Emperor Claudius begins the occupation of England.

c AD50 Just to the east of the modern London Bridge, the first wooden bridge over the Thames is constructed. The Roman historian Tacitus describes Londinium (a name which may have derived from the Celtic Llyn-din, the fort by the lake) as a thriving centre of trade.

AD61 Queen Boadicea's Iceni tribe burns London to the ground, but the town is immediately reconquered and remains under Roman rule for a further 350 years.

2nd century The area now known as the City is surrounded by a town wall. London develops into a prosperous town. All the roads built for the Roman armies, some of which extend as far as the Scottish border, start from London.

287 Roman admiral Carausius declares London's independence from the Roman Empire and establishes London as the capital.

296 Carausius's successor is defeated by forces loyal to the emperor and Roman rule is restored.

c 450 Roman legions withdraw from Britain and Angles, Saxons and Jutes invade, reducing the importance of London.

597 The Benedictine monk, Augustine, comes to Britain as a missionary 'to make angels out of the Angles'. Christianity arrives in England.

610 St Paul's Cathedral becomes the seat of the Bishop of London.

796 Anglo Saxons establish London as the seat of the king.

799–896 Vikings raid and plunder London.

884 Alfred the Great declares London the capital of the kingdom.

1016–35 The Danish King Canute rules England. London has to pay dues of £10,500, an indication of the wealth of the town at that time.

1066–87 William the Conqueror, Duke of Normandy, defeats King Harold II at the Battle of Hastings and is crowned as the first King of England in Westminster Abbey. London Bridge is built and remains the only link between the north and south banks of the Thames until 1750.

1087 Fire destroys St Paul's Cathedral and a large part of the City.

1136 London Bridge has to be rebuilt after another fire. With 19 arches and huge piers, it creates such a swell of water that it becomes impossible for boats to pass under it. Until it is dismantled in 1880, boats have to be lifted out of the water and then returned on the other side of the bridge.

1189–99 In return for a payment of £1,500, Richard I grants the citizens of London a charter, which guarantees their rights to the Thames.

1191–1212 Henry Fitz Aylwin becomes London's first elected mayor, testifying to the growing power of the guilds.

1215 The Magna Carta lays down the privileges of the City of London and the citizens' right to elect their own Lord Mayor is established, but he has still to be approved by the king. The modern 'Lord Mayor's Show' ceremony is an observance which dates back to the charter which required the mayor to be presented to the monarch.

1272–1307 Under Edward I, the first law schools (Inns of Court) are established. The clergy are banned from the law courts.

15th century The powerful guilds give London a tremendous boost and it becomes one of the biggest and most prosperous cities in Europe.

1509–47 Henry VIII breaks with the Catholic Church and founds the Anglican Church. Major changes to the religious and social framework result. The link between the state and the church is severed and many monasteries are destroyed.

1553–58 Queen Mary I (Bloody Mary), a fanatical Catholic, orders the execution of the Anglican Archbishop Cranmer and other supporters of the Anglican Church.

1558–1603 Queen Elizabeth I restores the Anglican Church, the arts and sciences flourish. The plays of Shakespeare and other playwrights of the time are performed in the Swan, the Rose and the famous Globe, all theatres on the south bank of the Thames. First water supply system installed.

1603 The Stuart King James I (James VI of Scotland) succeeds to the throne. Disputes with Puritans, a strong parliamentary presence, lead in 1605 to the Gunpowder Plot in which Guy Fawkes and his Catholic conspirators unsuccessfully attempt to blow up king and parliament.

1649–60 Charles I ignores the demands of parliament, dissolves the lower house and plunges the country into civil war. He is beheaded before the Banqueting Hall in Whitehall. A republic is declared. Oliver Cromwell becomes Lord Protector and takes up residence in Whitehall. Cromwell dies in 1658 and his son Richard succeeds him but resigns in 1659. In 1660 Charles II succeeds to the throne and the monarchy is restored.

1665 The Great Plague sweeps through London and the rest of the country, killing 90,000. The Dutch fleet sails up the Thames estuary and sinks the English navy.

1666 The Great Fire of London destroys four-fifths of the city. Architect Sir Christopher Wren submits a plan for rebuilding the city within days of the fire but his ideas are rejected. Eventually he goes ahead with his plans for the new St Paul's Cathedral. He plays an important part in the construction of another 320 churches.

1683 Charles II tries to undermine London's ancient privileges by replacing the elected councillors with royal officials.

1688 James II restores London's special privileges. The remains of the city walls which separated the wealthy City from the rest of London are demolished and the suburbs are extended. William of Orange and a powerful army land on the coast of England. James II, who tried to restore the Catholic religion, is forced into exile. The East India Company is established and trade with the rest of the world brings greater prosperity to the capital.

1718 The Quadruple Alliance is signed at an international conference in London uniting Britain, France, Austria and Holland.

1750 A second river crossing, Westminster Bridge, is completed.

1801 The first census puts the number of London's inhabitants at 860,035.

1806 London's pre-eminence as a trading centre suffers from the imposition of Napoleon I's Continental System which attempts to exclude British trade from mainland Europe.

1836 London's first railway line opens between London Bridge and Deptford.

1837–1901 London benefits from the stability provided by Queen Victoria's 64-year reign.

In **1851** (Great Exhibition) and **1862** (International Exhibition), the first worldwide exhibitions of their kind, take place in London.

1863 London's first underground line opens between Paddington and Farringdon Street.

1914–18 German air attacks on the city during World War I kill 670 Londoners.

1939–45 German air attacks on London kill 30,000 people. In the Square Mile (the financial area), nearly all houses and churches are destroyed or badly damaged during the Blitz.

1952 Elizabeth II succeeds to the throne.

1963 Reorganisation of local government creates the Greater London Council as the upper tier of London administration, embracing the 32 boroughs and the City of London.

1973 Tower Bridge is fitted with an electrical lifting mechanism and becomes a museum. Great Britain joins the European Community.

1979 Margaret Thatcher becomes the first woman prime minister. Her economic policies, now usually described as Thatcherism, seek to restrain public spending and transfer state-owned industries to the private sector.

1981 Prince Charles marries Lady Diana Spencer in St Paul's Cathedral. Work begins on the massive redevelopment of the Docklands area.

1982 The Barbican Centre conference and arts centre is opened by Queen Elizabeth II.

1984 The Thames Flood Barrier, built to protect low-lying parts of London, is opened.

1986 The Greater London Council is abolished, leaving London with no elected city government.

1990 John Major becomes prime minister and goes on to win the 1992 general election.

1992 In November, a fire badly damages parts of Windsor Castle.

1993 Britain ratifies the Maastricht Treaty.

1994 The Channel Tunnel opens, linking London with Paris and Brussels.

The Kings and Queens of England

Anglo-Saxons
827–839 Egbert, King of Wessex
839–856 Ethelwulf
866–871 Ethelred I
871–899 Alfred the Great
899–924 Edward the Elder
924–940 Athelstan
959–975 Edgar
975–978 Edmund the Martyr
978–1016 Ethelred the Unready
1016 Edward the Ironside
1042–1066 Edward the Confessor
1066 Harold II

Danes
1016–1035 Canute the Dane
1035–1040 Harold I
1041–1042 Hardicanute

Normans
1066–1087 William the Conqueror
1087–1100 William II
1100–1135 Henry I
1135–1154 Stephen, Count of Blois

Plantagenets
1154–1189 Henry II
1189–1199 Richard I
1199–1216 John
1216–1272 Henry III
1272–1307 Edward I
1307–1327 Edward II
1327–1377 Edward III
1377–1399 Richard II

House of Lancaster
1399–1413 Henry IV
1413–1422 Henry V
1422–1461 Henry VI

House of York
1461–1483 Edward IV
1483 Edward V
1483–1485 Richard III

Tudors
1485–1509 Henry VII
1509–1547 Henry VIII
1547–1553 Edward VI
1553–1558 Mary I
1558–1603 Elizabeth I

Stuarts
1603–1625 James I
1625–1649 Charles I
1649–1660 Cromwell's Commonwealth
1660–1685 Charles II
1685–1688 James II
1688–1694 William III and Mary II
1694–1702 William III
1702–1714 Anne

House of Hanover
1714–1727 George I
1727–1760 George II
1760–1820 George III
1820–1830 George IV
1830–1837 William IV
1837–1901 Victoria

House of Saxe-Coburg
1901–1910 Edward VII

House of Windsor
1910–1936 George V
1936–1952 George VI
1952–   Elizabeth II

Preceding pages:
City on the Thames

Eros' cupid

Madame Tussaud's Rock Circus

Route 1

★★ **Piccadilly Circus – Pall Mall – Trafalgar Square – ★★National Gallery – Whitehall – ★ Houses of Parliament – ★★★ Westminster Abbey – ★ Buckingham Palace – St James's Park – Burlington Arcade**

This route takes in London's main sights, beginning at ★★ **Piccadilly Circus ❶** (nearest Underground station: *Piccadilly Circus*), which is generally regarded as the centre of London. In the middle of the circus is Eros – officially the Angel of Charity – a memorial, dating from 1893, to the philanthropist Lord Shaftesbury. A short distance from Eros is the Trocadero shopping and entertainments centre in Coventry Street with the Guinness World of Records exhibition. Madame Tussaud's Rock Circus, also in Piccadilly Circus, gives an insight into the glitzy world of rock and pop stars.

At the Piccadilly Circus Underground station, the biggest in London, turn right off Coventry Street into the Haymarket for the **Design Council ❷** (*see page 84*) and the Haymarket Theatre with its fine Georgian facade.

The Haymarket leads to **Pall Mall**, the elegant headquarters of London's clubland. A little further on to the right in Waterloo Place ❸ stands the **Crimea Monument**, a memorial to the dead of the Crimean War. Several other memorials have found their home here, including the 120ft (40m) Duke of York's column. **St James's Square ❹**

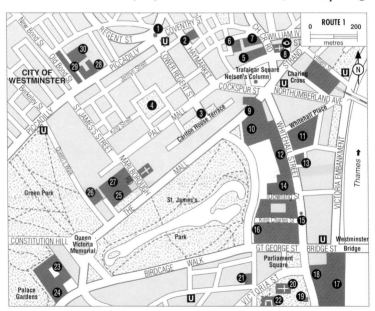

dates from the 17th century and has some fine Georgian town houses and the equestrian statue of William III.

Feeding time

Turn left along Pall Mall towards the famous **Trafalgar Square** (nearest Underground station: *Charing Cross*). The square is named after Admiral Nelson's victory over the combined Spanish and French navy off Cape Trafalgar on 21 October 1805. The 160-ft (55-m) high Nelson's Column was completed in 1843. The bronze reliefs cast from French cannon show scenes from Nelson's victorious battles. The other monuments and bronze busts show English generals and admirals. Trafalgar Square is a popular meeting place for tourists and huge numbers of pigeons. But the most famous gathering in Trafalgar Square is on New Year's Eve when thousands of revellers welcome in the New Year.

Sculpture in the square

15

On the northern side of square is the impressive façade of the ★★**National Gallery ❺**.

It was built between 1834 and 1837 and is certainly the one London art gallery which should not be missed. It houses one of the most extensive and valuable collections of paintings in the world. Nearly all the European painting movements are represented by the 4,500 works, some dating from the 13th century. The highlights are works by Rembrandt, Rubens, Dürer, Raphael, Titian, Leonardo da Vinci, El Greco, Murillo, Velázquez, Constable, Gainsborough, Cézanne, Degas, Manet, Rossetti and many others. In 1991 the Sainsbury Wing was opened, giving the gallery some much-needed extra space.

The National's Sainsbury Wing

Behind the National Gallery is the **Central Reference Library ❻** and the **National Portrait Gallery ❼** (nearest Underground stations: *Charing Cross* or *Leicester Square*). This gallery contains more than 4,500 portraits of celebrated personalities from British history, literature, art and science and includes the work of Reynolds, Lawrence, Godfrey Kneller and Constable.

The columns of St Martin

Posing with the guards

Only a few yards away, also on the northern side of Trafalgar Square, is **St Martin-in-the-Fields** ❽. Built by James Gibbs between 1721 and 1726, this famous church stands on the site of a medieval chapel. As well as designing an unusual 170-ft (56-m) steeple, Gibbs set an outstanding Corinthian portico before the west front. In the nave stands a font which has survived from the first church. St Martin's stands within the parish of the British Admiralty and Buckingham Palace. In the crypt is a café, a shop and a brass rubbing centre, where for a small fee it is possible to copy replicas of brasses from all over the country and from abroad.

Alongside the church is Trafalgar Square post office. From the southwest corner of the square runs The Mall, an imposing boulevard laid out in 1660 which leads to Buckingham Palace (*see page 21*). Pass first under the massive **Admiralty Arch** ❾, which was built in 1910 to commemorate the reign of Queen Victoria. Directly behind it is the **British Admiralty** ❿, a domed building dating from the turn of the century. Running south from Trafalgar Square is Whitehall, where most of the British government's ministerial offices are situated. On the left-hand side of the road is the **War Office** ⓫ with an equestrian statue of the Duke of Cambridge, who was Commander-in-Chief of the British forces for 40 years.

On the right is the Old Admiralty and the **Horse Guards** ⓬ (nearest Underground station: *Charing Cross*). The changing of the guard takes place at 11am (Sunday 10am). A military presence is maintained by two sentries from the Household Cavalry, who sit silent and motionless as the tourists' cameras whirr. The Trooping of the Colour, in honour of the Queen's birthday, takes place here in June. Opposite the Horse Guards is the **Banqueting House** ⓭ (Tuesday to Saturday 10am–5pm, Sunday 2–5pm), a superb example of Palladian-style architecture built by Inigo Jones in 1619 and still used for official receptions. In 1635 Charles I commissioned Rubens to paint the nine sumptuous ceiling paintings which are in the first-floor rooms. Above the entrance stands a bust of Charles I, marking the spot where he stepped on to the scaffold on 30 January 1649 (*see page 10*).

Continuing down Whitehall, on the right just past the Treasury, the narrow street to the right now blocked off to the public is **Downing Street** ⓮ and the official residence of the Prime Minister at number 10. Number 11 is the home of the Chancellor of the Exchequer, the British finance minister. There are a number of other government offices in Downing Street. On an island in the middle of Whitehall is the **Cenotaph** ⓯, the national memorial (1920) to British forces who have died in action and the focus of Remeberence Sunday services each November.

At the end of King Charles Street are the **Cabinet War Rooms** . These rooms were the underground sanctuary for Winston Churchill and his cabinet during the air raids of World War II. They have been left untouched since the end of the war and may be visited (daily 10am–5.50pm). The rest of Whitehall is also known as Parliament Street and leads to Parliament Square with its monuments of famous British politicians.

Parliament was rebuilt in 1834
Cabinet War Rooms

Officially known as the Palace of Westminster, the ★ **Houses of Parliament** ⓱ (nearest Underground station: *Westminster*) stand on the site of the royal palace of Edward the Confessor (1042–66). In 1547 it became the seat of parliament, but was completely rebuilt in neo-Gothic style after the 1834 fire, and named the New Palace of Westminster.

The buildings contain more than 1,100 rooms grouped around 11 courtyards. Frescoes, carvings, coats of arms, portraits and statues of Norman rulers, British monarchs and important statesmen and women adorn the corridors and lobbies. For security reasons, the Houses of Parliament are not accessible to the general public. Visits can be arranged only by the invitation of a Member of Parliament. It is, however, possible to witness sessions in the House of Commons (lower house) and House of Lords (upper house) from the Visitors' Gallery and thereby gain an insight into the British parliamentary system. In order to gain entry, which is free, visitors should wait at the entrance by St Stephen's Hall, south of Westminster Hall (see below), on Monday to Thursday from 4.15pm and on Friday from 10am. For the House of Lords, the hours are Monday to Wednesday from 2.30pm, Thursday from 3pm and Friday from 11am.

The **House of Commons** lies behind Westminster Hall. In 1852 Sir George Gilbert Scott redesigned the building in Early Gothic style. It was destroyed by fire after

Westminster Hall

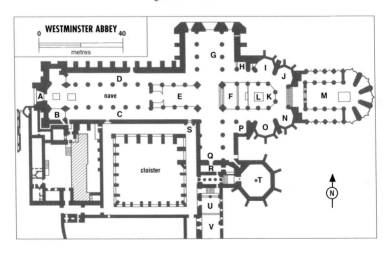

*The most famous clock in
the world*

an air attack in 1941, but was rebuilt without decoration. The chamber has seats for only 437 Members of Parliament out of a total of 650. The Prime Minister and his cabinet ministers sit facing the opposition ministers.

The **House of Lords** is situated to the south. In contrast to the House of Commons, it is a grandly decorated hall with encrusted gold, gilt and scarlet. In front of the two thrones for the king and queen are the Woolsack, the traditional seat of the Lord Chancellor.

To the west of the Houses of Parliament stands ★★◢ **Westminster Hall** ⓲. This is the oldest part of Westminster Palace and measures 250ft (79m) by 70ft (22m) reaching a height of 100ft (30m). Commissioned by William II it was built between 1097 and 1099. It also suffered a serious fire, but Richard II rebuilt it at the end of the 14th century. From the 13th century right up until 1825, Westminster Hall was the seat of England's highest court. Many ceremonial occasions, including coronations, have been held here. As at the Houses of Parliament, visits can be arranged only through a Member of Parliament. The highlight of the interior is the hammerbeam roof, regarded by some as the finest timber roof ever built.

Another famous landmark is the 300-ft (97-m) **Clock Tower** at the north end of the Palace of Westminster. The 13-ton bell, usually known as **Big Ben**, is recognised throughout the world as the 'sound of London' and British people invariably set their watches by its chimes. Each of the four clockfaces is 23ft (8m) in diameter.

On the opposite side of the road is the ★ **Jewel Tower** ⓳, which was built in 1366 and used as a strongroom for Edward III's jewels and treasure. It subsequently became the archive for parliamentary papers and then the weights and measures office. It is now a museum.

One of the finest sights in England is ★★★ **Westminster Abbey** ⓴ (nearest underground stations: *Westminster* or *St James's Park*). Abbey: 8am–6pm, Wednesday to 7.45pm. Choir and sanctuary: admittance until 45 minutes before closing Monday to Friday 9.20am–4pm, Saturday 9.20am–2pm and 3.45–5pm. Chapter House mid-March to mid-October daily: 9.30am–6pm, mid-October to mid-March 9.30am–4pm. Museum and Chapel of the Pyx: daily 10.30am–4pm. For times of services, tel: 0171-222 5152. No parties are admitted into the church during services. Tour with guide April–October Monday to Friday at 10am, 10.30am, 11am, 2pm, 2.30pm, 3pm, Saturday at 10am, 11am, 12.30pm, November–March at 10am, 11am, 2pm, 3pm, Saturday at 10am, 11am, 12.30pm.

Edward the Confessor founded Westminster Abbey in the 11th century on the site of an old Benedictine abbey dating from 750. Since William the Conqueror in 1066, every king or queen of England has been crowned in Westminster Abbey. Most monarchs and their families from Henry II to George II are buried here. The abbey is 500ft (170m) long and 75ft (25m) wide and has the highest Gothic nave in England (100ft/34m).

The best place to start a tour of the abbey is at the west door [A], from where the triple-naved interior with its examples of all three English Gothic styles (Early English, Decorated, Perpendicular) may be admired. The Tomb of the Unknown Warrior lies inside the west door.

Immediately to the right, in the southwest corner, is St George's Chapel [B], which is dedicated to the dead of World War I. A portrait of Richard II (1377–99) hangs on one of the pillars and is the oldest portrait of an English monarch in existence.

The south aisle [C] is adorned with plaques and monuments to British artists, scientists and travellers. Along the north aisle [D], however, politicians, musicians and

The north facade of Westminster Abbey

19

The west facade

some scientists such as Lord Lister, Charles Darwin and Isaac Newton are remembered.

Despite numerous alterations to the abbey, the choir [E] occupies the same position as it did in Edward the Confessor's reign and in Norman times when the abbey was completed. The 13th-century Gothic pews were destroyed in 1775 and were replaced in 1834.

Look for the remarkable large rose windows in the transept. It is in the Sanctuary [F] where the kings and queens are crowned. To the left are the three medieval gravestones of Edmund Crouchback (1296), his wife, Aveline (1273) and Aymer de Valence (1324).

Over to the right is an ancient 13th-century sedilia (priest's chair), painted with full-length royal figures, and also the grave of Anne of Cleves, Henry VIII's fourth wife, who died in 1557. The high altar dates from 1867 and is the work of Sir Gilbert Scott. The north transept [G] contains mainly tombstones, plaques and monuments to famous British statesmen.

To view the royal chapels, start at the north side. On the lower floor of the Chapel of Abbot Islip [H] is the grave of John Islip, the church architect, who died in 1532. To the right is the Chapel of St John the Baptist [I] and St Paul's Chapel [J]. On the right, to the south of the chapel, is Henry V's chantry chapel [K] with the tomb of Henry V [L], which lies on the site of the old Saxon church's apse. The famous Chapel of Edward the Confessor, who died in 1066 (although the chapel was not completed until 1268), lies between Henry V's tomb and the Coronation Chair. The chair, which is made of oak, is moved into the sanctuary for coronations. It encloses the Stone of Some, a block of reddish sandstone. It was first used by the Scots for their own coronations, before being carried off by Edward I in 1297 for the same use in England.

Fan-vaulted roof of the Henry VII Chapel

Some steps lead up to the Henry VII Chapel [M], which dates from the beginning of the 16th century, and is magnificently decorated. The fan-vaulted roof is a superb example of Late Perpendicular style. The chapel consists of a nave, two aisles and five smaller chapels. Henry VII and Elizabeth of York are buried here (behind the altar), Mary Stuart (in the southern aisle) and Elizabeth I (in the northern aisle).

The Royal Airforce Chapel is dedicated to the dead of World War II. The windows show the colours of the 63rd bomber squadron which took part in the Battle of Britain in 1940. St Nicholas's Chapel [N] on the south side contains tombstones from the 15th to 17th century and in St Edmund's Chapel [O] is the remarkably carved tombstone of William de Valence (1296).

The alabaster tomb of Simon Langham (1376), Lord Chancellor and Archbishop of Canterbury, occupies the next chapel, St Benedict's [P]. The south transept [Q] contains the tombstones, busts and plaques of over 100 poets and writers, in Poets' Corner. To the rear is St Faith's Chapel [R], with a magnificent Brussels tapestry.

A door [S] leads from the south transept into the cloisters. On the northern side is some fine 13th-century stonework. The octagonal Chapter House [T] built between 1245 and 1255, with vaulting spreading from a single central pier, was once used as a royal treasury. The ribbing around the six 40-ft (13-m) high windows is the earliest example of Early Decorated style. The well-maintained 13th-century floor tiles are particularly interesting, as are the tapestry, the circular tympanum above the door and the 3rd-century Roman sarcophagus with a carved Saxon cross in the porch. Between 1352 and 1547, the English parliament met in the Chapter House.

Formerly the vestry, the Chamber of the Pyx [U], with its fine Norman doorway, was converted into the monastery treasury, where gold and silver coins were checked against standard specimens that were kept in a box (pyx).

Finally, the Abbey Museum is housed in the 11th-century Norman undercroft or crypt [V]. Exhibits include documents, gold plate, replicas of coronation regalia and a number of unique wax and wood effigies.

Close by is the domed **Central Hall** ㉑, centre of the Methodist Church (*see page 7*), and **Church House** ㉒, administrative seat of the Church of England.

St James's Park is the oldest and probably the most delightful of London's parks. From the bridge, there is a fine view of Buckingham Palace and Whitehall.

The cloisters
The Chapter House

Buckingham Palace from
St James's Park

Marching for the Queen

Queen Victoria Memorial

Museum of Mankind exhibit

To the west (*see map on page 14*) is ★ **Buckingham Palace** ㉓, the Queen's main residence. The palace, built in 1703, was later completely rebuilt and enlarged by John Nash from 1824–30. The east front, a 360-ft (120-m) long facade in classical style, was completed in 1913. If the Queen is at home, the Royal Standard flag flies over the palace. Since 1993, visitors have been admitted on a tour during several weeks each August and September, although the Queen is not in residence at the time. Open daily 9.30am–5.30pm; tickets available on the corner of St James's Park opposite the palace.

The changing of the guard takes place daily at 11.30am, but on alternate days between September and March, affairs of state and weather permitting.

The **Queen's Gallery** ㉔ (nearest Underground station: *Victoria*) displays exhibitions from the Royal Collection including paintings, drawings and furniture.

From the 1911 Queen Victoria Memorial in front of Buckingham Palace, follow The Mall in a northeasterly direction (*see page 14*). To the left are **Clarence House** ㉕, the Queen Mother's official residence and ★ **Lancaster House** ㉖, the opulent residence of the Duke of York and a centre for banquets and state receptions.

We soon come to ★ **St James's Palace** ㉗. This brick palace commissioned by Henry VIII to Holbein's plans was the official residence of the royal family from 1698 to 1837, and is today the London residence of Prince Charles. The gateway leads to the 17th-century colonnade of the Colour Court, but the state rooms are not open to the public.

St James's Street has many fine 18th-century houses and leading off to the right is Jermyn Street, famous for its high-class shirt and shoe shops.

Piccadilly runs parallel, slightly further to the north. **Burlington House** ㉘ with its neo-Renaissance facade (1847) is the home of the Academy, where painters such as Reynolds, Constable, Turner, Lawrence and Millais either studied or taught. The Academy regularly holds exhibitions of paintings and sculptures by contemporary artists. Its annual Summer Exhibition, to which anybody may submit work, is regarded as a social highlight. To the west, the building adjoins the **Burlington Arcade** ㉙, an 1819 shopping mall with 72 fashionable shops. Parallel to Burlington Arcade is Bond Street, another high-class shopping street with many jewellers, fashion houses and galleries.

The **Museum of Mankind** ㉚ is the ethnographical department of the British Museum, and holds some outstanding exhibitions depicting the cultures of Africa, Australia and the Pacific Islands, North and South America and parts of Asia and Europe (*see page 73*).

Route 2

Covent Garden capers

Trafalgar Square – Covent Garden – Royal Courts of Justice – ★ The Temple – ★★ St Paul's Cathedral

From **Trafalgar Square ㉛** (*see page 15*) follow Duncannon Street past St Martin-in-the-Fields (*see page 16*) to the Strand and **Charing Cross ㉜**. The village of Charing once stood on the spot where Edward I placed the last of 13 crosses marking the route of his wife Eleanor's funeral cortège from Harby in Nottinghamshire to Westminster Abbey. The modern cross is a replica of the original. The bronze plaque behind the equestrian statue of Charles I (1675) is regarded as the official centre of London and all distances from London are measured from this point. Charing Cross Station (1864) is an important station serving southern and southeast England.

Up the Garden path

The Strand is a busy shopping street. Its name is derived from the fact that during Tudor times the gardens of the town houses on the southern side of the street stretched down to the banks of the Thames. **St Paul's Church ㉝** in Bedford Street was built in 1633 by Inigo Jones in neoclassical style, but it was badly damaged by fire and rebuilt in 1798. This church has always been closely associated with actors, artists, musicians and craftsmen and many of them were buried there during the 18th and 19th centuries.

Covent Garden ㉞, made famous by the musical *My Fair Lady*, was for 300 years London's flower and vegetable market. The old market has been transformed into a lively shopping precinct and a centre for art galleries. The Royal Opera House, London Transport Museum and Theatre Museum are within a few hundred yards (*see pages 76, 73, 75*). Return to the Strand and turn right into Savoy Street to find the **Queen's Chapel of the Savoy ㉟**,

Courtauld Institute Galleries

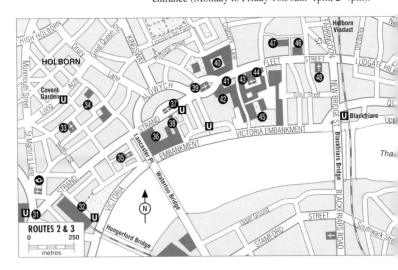

Justice prevails

dating from 1505. Destroyed by fire, it was restored in Perpendicular style in 1864.

The impressive **Somerset House 36** has served many purposes since it was built by Sir William Chambers at the end of the 18th century, but the 700-ft (200-m) riverside facade is one of the finest in Britain. Built on the site of a former royal palace, it now houses the ★★ **Courtauld Institute Galleries**, with a collection of Impressionist and post-Impressionist paintings by Manet, Degas, Monet, Renoir, Seurat, Cézanne, van Gogh. Works by Botticelli, Bellini, Veronese, Tintoretto, Rubens and Goya are also exhibited here (*see page 72*).

On an island in the middle of the Strand, with traffic flowing either side, is the **church of Mary-le-Strand 37** (nearest Underground station: *Aldwych*), which was built by James Gibbs between 1714 and 1717 and is noted in particular for its fine coffered plaster ceiling.

The **Roman Bath 38** was founded in Tudor times and is fed by a nearby spring. The address is 5 Strand Lane and it can usually be viewed through the window.

St Clement Danes 39 was built in 1681 by Sir Christopher Wren, and although it was destroyed in World War II, it has been faithfully restored. It is believed that Danish settlers lived on the original site of the church. A carillon bell rings out the famous nursery rhyme ('Oranges and lemons, sing the bells of St Clements') at 9am, noon, 3pm and 6pm. Nowadays the church is dedicated to the Royal Air Force. To the left can be seen the distinctive white facade of the **Royal Courts of Justice 40**, England and Wales's highest civil court. There is a small exhibition of legal costumes situated close to the main entrance (Monday to Friday 10.30am–1pm, 2–4pm).

Temple Bar Memorial ❹ was constructed in 1880 on the site of the old customs gate. The monument surmounted by a griffin marks the boundary between Westminster and the City of London.

City boundary

Fleet Street is just inside the City boundary. Its name derives from the River Fleet which now flows beneath the street. Fleet Street was once the centre of the British newspaper industry, but many of the major publishers have moved their offices and printing presses to Docklands. The centuries-old tradition of printing in this area is over, and the 'Street of Ink and Adventure' is now just another street of shops and offices.

Before continuing along Fleet Street, it is worth taking a look at **Prince Henry's Room** ❷, which is contained in a timber-framed building (1611) with an overhanging first floor. The room is thought to be the place where Prince Henry, James I's older son, met with the Council of the Duchy of Cornwall. The oak panelling and Jacobean ceiling bearing the prince's initials are original and date from the 17th century.

At the start of Fleet Street is ★ **The Temple** ❸ (nearest Underground station: *Temple*). The site dates to the 12th century when it was acquired by the order of Templars. In 1312, when the order was suppressed, the land was assigned to the crown, but eventually fell into the hands of the lawyers to whom it had been leased previously. Thus the Temple became the headquarters of the English legal profession and has remained so. Many of London's top barristers and lawyers have their offices in the vicinity.

Temple Church ❹ is one of the few remaining round churches. It dates from the 12th and 13th centuries and the

Inside Temple Church

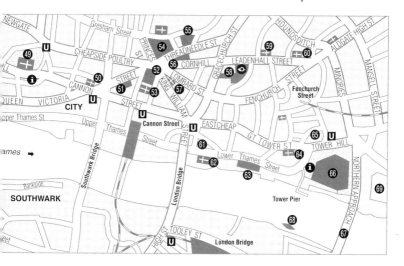

choir (1240) is a superb example of the Early English style. In 1682, Sir Christopher Wren rebuilt a section of the church, and although it suffered badly in World War II, it was carefully restored in 1954.

It is well worth taking a stroll through the Inner Temple and into the **Temple Gardens** 🅰, which extend as far as the bank of the Thames. On the left side of Fleet Street is the Wine Office Court with the famous pub **Ye Olde Cheshire Cheese** 🅱 which dates from 1667. Many celebrated figures from English literary history, such as Johnson, Boswell and Goldsmith, met here.

Dr Samuel Johnson

A narrow alley leads to **Dr Johnson's House** 🅲 where the 18th-century critic and lexicographer Dr Samuel Johnson lived from 1748 to 1759. It was here that he wrote his *Dictionary* and magazine *The Rambler*. (Monday to Friday 11am–5.30pm, in winter 11am–5pm). At the eastern end of Fleet Street is **St Bride's** 🅳, the journalists' church. Built by Wren at the end of the 17th century on the site of an older church, much of it was destroyed in World War II. The wedding-cake steeple (1701) survived but the rest of the church has been faithfully restored. The fascinating Crypt Museum (open daily 8.15am–5.30pm) is a magpie collection of Roman mosaics, Saxon church walls and William Caxton's *Ovid*.

The dome of St Paul's

We now come to **★★ St Paul's Cathedral** 🅴 (nearest Underground station: *St Paul's*). The cathedral is open daily 9.30am–4.30pm (apart from during services); galleries Monday to Saturday 9.30am–4.30pm; crypt open at around 11am. Guided tours are available Monday to Saturday 11am, 11.30am, 2pm, 2.30pm.

The cathedral, the seat of the Bishop of London, is Sir Christopher Wren's masterpiece. It was built between 1675 and 1710 on the site of a medieval church destroyed in the

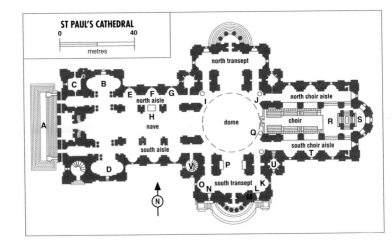

ST PAUL'S CATHEDRAL

0   40

metres

north transept

C   B

E   F   G

north aisle   I   J

north choir aisle

H

nave   dome   choir   R   S

A   Q

south aisle   south choir aisle

T

D   V   P   U

O   south transept   L   K

N   M

N

Great Fire of 1666. Its most striking ground-level feature is the two-tier portico (180ft/60m), but it is the 350ft-(111-m) dome which characterises St Paul's. Crowned by a golden cross, it dominates the skyline.

Enter the cathedral by two wide flights of marble steps [A]. Just inside on the left is St Dunstan's Chapel [B] with a finely carved oak screen dating from the 17th century and also All Souls' Chapel [C], a memorial (1916) to Earl Kitchener, the British war minister who died when his ship was sunk on its way to Russia. On the opposite side is St Michael and St George's Chapel [D] with a memorial to Lord Forrest, an Australian peer who died in 1918. In the north aisle, alongside the graves of painter Lord Leighton [E], General Gordon [F] and Viscount Melbourne [G], stands the Wellington Monument [H]. Also in the north aisle are statues of the painter Joshua Reynolds [I] and the writer and critic Dr Samuel Johnson [J].

Cathedral nave

In the south aisle are monuments to Admiral Earl Howe [K], Admiral Collingwood [L], J M W Turner [M], Sir John Moore [N] and General Abercromby [O], all dating from the beginning of the 19th century. Note the four symbolic pictures (*North Sea*, *Baltic*, *Mediterranean* and *Nile*) around the fine portrait statue of Lord Nelson [P].

27

In front of the choir stalls is a splendid oak pulpit [Q]. The stalls themselves (17th-century) are the work of Grinling Gibbons. A World War II bomb destroyed the High Altar [R] and in 1958 a new marble altar was constructed. Behind it is the American Chapel of Remembrance [S], which contains the names of 25,000 American soldiers who died defending Britain during World War II.

Statue of John Donne

In the south choir aisle is the statue of John Donne [T], poet and Dean of St Paul's from 1621 to 1623. It stands on an urn wrapped in his shroud and it is the only statue which was saved from the fire which destroyed the old St Paul's.

At the western end of the choir aisle is the Dean's pulpit [U], from where a staircase leads to the crypt. Men of all talents are buried here, including Lord Nelson, J M W Turner, Joshua Reynolds and Sir Alexander Fleming. The simple grave of Sir Christopher Wren bears the Latin inscription: *Lector, si monumentum requiris, circumspice* (Reader, if you seek his monument, look around you).

There are a number of galleries in the dome and they can be reached via the staircase at the southwest pillar [V]. The famous Whispering Gallery, whose acoustic qualities have encouraged generations of schoolchildren to giggle secret messages, offers unusual perspectives of the choir and the arches and also a close-up of the interior of the dome. The prospect from the Golden Gallery at the top of the dome is better than from the Stone Gallery as it allows a fine view over London, towering above most of the tall buildings which now surround the cathedral.

Route 3

Mansion House – ★Monument – ★★★ Tower of London – St Katharine's Dock

After visiting St Paul's (*see page 26*), take a walk around the building to get an impression of the construction work that is taking place in this part of London (*see map on pages 24–25*). Paternoster Square to the north of St Paul's is being redesigned but in a style which matches the majesty of Sir Christopher Wren's masterpiece. From the east of the cathedral, follow Cannon Street as far as Queen Victoria Street.

On the left is **St Mary Aldermary** ⑤⓪, which Wren rebuilt after the fire (1682) using remains of the destroyed shell to create a replica of the original. It is unusual in that it was one of the few churches which Wren built in a neo-Gothic style.

In Queen Victoria Street is the Bucklersbury House office block, only of interest because it stands on the site of the **Mithras Temple** ⑤① (nearest Underground station: *Bank*). Built around the year AD90, the temple is in the outline of a basilica and was discovered in 1954 when foundations were being dug for the office block.

The **Mansion House** ⑤② is the official residence of the Lord Mayor of London. It was built between 1739 and 1753 by George Dance in Renaissance style with a raised portico of six giant Corinthian columns. The church of **St Stephen Walbrook** ⑤③ is adjacent. St Paul's, which it pre-dates, was in some ways modelled on it. The 65-ft (21-m) dome rests on a ring of eight circular arches, in turn supported by Corinthian columns.

The **Bank of England** ⑤④ (nearest Underground station: *Bank*) is one of the world's leading banks. This striking building was built between 1788 and 1833 by Sir John Soane, but in the 1920s it was rebuilt to plans by Sir Herbert Baker. The elegant curtain wall was planned with security in mind. The Bank of England Museum provides a fascinating insight into the 300-year history of this institution (Monday to Friday 10am–5pm; from Easter until the end of September also Sundays 11am–5pm). In neighbouring Threadneedle Street is the **London Stock Exchange** ⑤⑤. Built in 1773, it fell into disuse after the so-called 'Big Bang' in 1986 which introduced electronic dealing systems.

Diagonally opposite is the **Royal Exchange** ⑤⑥, which was rebuilt in the middle of the 19th century on the site of the two previous exchanges, both of which were destroyed by fire (1666 and 1838). It now boasts a monumental Corinthian portico. One unusual feature is the famous carillon, which at 9am, noon, 3pm and 6pm plays

Seal of approval

Inside St Stephen's

The Royal Exchange

English, Scottish, Welsh, Canadian and Australian folk tunes. The oldest part of the building is the central court-yard with an arcade at ground-floor and first-floor levels where the merchants used to congregate. Nearby is the beautiful church of **St Mary Woolnoth** ⑤⑦, which was built between 1716 and 1727.

Follow Cornhill Street with Wren's St Peter's upon Cornhill and St Michael's Cornhill as far as Gracechurch Street. Turn right into **Leadenhall Market** ⑤⑧. Towering above is Richard Rogers's futuristic Lloyd's building (open only for tours on application).

Welcome to Lloyd's

It is worth making a short detour along Leadenhall Street to the church of **St Andrew Undershaft** ⑤⑨ to see a monument by Nicholas Stone of the antiquarian John Stow and a plaque in the south aisle to the German painter Hans Holbein the Younger who died of the plague in London in 1543. A little further on is the church of **St Katherine Cree** ⑥⓪.

Follow Fenchurch Street southwards and into Gracechurch Street to reach Monument Street and the ★ **Monument** ⑥① (nearest Underground station: *Monument*). The 200-ft (67-m) tall column of Portland stone was built by Wren as the 'highest freestanding column in the world', to commemorate the victims of the Great Fire of 1666. A spiral staircase leads to a platform which offers a panorama (April–September Monday to Friday 9am–5.40pm, Saturday and Sunday 2–5.40pm, October–March Monday to Saturday 9am–4pm).

Pass the church of **St Magnus the Martyr** ⑥② , also by Wren, and follow Lower Thames Street eastwards to-

29

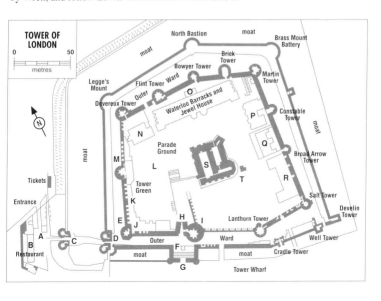

wards the **Custom House** 🅱, a 500-ft (170-m) wide building dating from the beginning of the 19th century. A left-turn into Byward Street leads to **All Hallows by the Tower** 🅱. Destroyed in World War II, this church has been almost completely rebuilt. Yet in the south wall of the tower is the only Anglo-Saxon arch still standing in the City – a relic from the first church to stand on this site, believed to have been built around 675. The brick tower, built only eight years before the Great Fire, was the only church tower in the City to survive. Some of the curiosities to be found in this church are a font carved from a piece of the Rock of Gibraltar (1944), a cross believed to have been brought back from Palestine by the Crusaders, and gravestones dating from the 15th and 17th centuries. These, plus the fact that this church has long been associated with the Toc H organisation and has a dedicated chapel with a Toc H lamp, give this church a distinctive atmosphere despite its obvious modern feel.

Detail of Trinity House

On **Trinity Square** 🅱 is the elegant Trinity House (1793), seat of the Corporation of Trinity House or the Brethren of the Trinity. Its charter dates from 1514 and it controls all sea-marks, lighthouses, lightships and pilotage. The huge headquarters of the Port of London Authority, which controls shipping on the Thames, dominates the square. To the west is Trinity Square Gardens where stood the scaffold to which prisoners from the Tower of London were brought for execution.

Some impressive Roman and medieval remains of London's city walls can be seen in 42 Trinity Square, in Midland House and in the nearby Cooper's Row.

Touring the Tower

We now come to the ★★★ **Tower of London** 🅱 (nearest Underground station: *Tower Hill*) Monday to Saturday 9.30am–5pm, Sunday 10am–5pm, November–February Monday to Saturday 9.30am–4pm.

This fortress by the Thames was built by William the Conqueror after the Battle of Hastings in 1066. Between the 12th and 14th centuries, it was rebuilt and extended. There is nothing at all left of the royal palace built by Henry I. It was as a jail that it became famous; prisoners included David II of Scotland (1346–57), James I of Scotland (1406–07), Henry IV (murdered 1471), Sir Thomas More (executed 1535), two of Henry VIII's wives: Anne Boleyn and Katherine Howard (executed 1536 and 1542 respectively), Elizabeth I (1554), Thomas Cromwell (executed 1540), Lady Jane Grey (executed 1554), William Penn (1668–69) and Rudolf Hess (1941).

The entrance to the Tower is in the southwest corner [A]. From the 14th century to 1834, the Lion Tower, which served as the royal menagerie, was situated here [B]. Pass through the 13th-century Middle Tower [C], rebuilt in the 18th century, to the Byward Tower [D], the 14th-century main gate where the portcullis lifting machinery is still in position on the first floor. The Bell Tower [E] is visible from the narrow outer court. Dating from the 12th century, this used to be the prison cell for royalty. Set in the outer wall opposite the large bastion is St Thomas's Tower [F]. This 12th-century tower contains an oratory named after the famous Archbishop of Canterbury Thomas Becket. The Traitors' Gate [G] was the entrance through which traitors and dissidents were brought in when the river was London's principal thoroughfare.

Guarding the nation's treasures

Once through the gate, prisoners would come face to face with the Bloody Tower [H], where many famous captives passed their final days. To the right stands the huge Wakefield Tower [I]. Built by Henry III, it was used to house state archives between 1360 and 1856.

In the southwest corner of the inner courtyard is a wooden house, known as the King's House [J] (or Queen's House). It was built in the reign of Henry VIII and is now the home of the Governor of the Tower of London. The 17th-century Gaoler's House [K] is adjacent. The western section of the inner courtyard is known as Tower Green [L] and the spot where many of the famous victims were executed is marked.

Graffiti left by prisoners

31

Built in the 13th century, Beauchamp Tower [M] contains a room on the first floor where it is still possible to see graffiti scratched on the wall by prisoners.

The Royal Chapel of St Peter ad Vincula [N] was founded in 1100, renovated in the 13th century and then completely rebuilt in 1512 after a fire. It is the burial place of the 'two dukes between the queens'. The Dukes of Somerset and Northumberland lie between two of Henry VIII's wives, Anne Boleyn and Katherine Howard. Lady Jane Grey and many others are also buried here. It may be visited only as part of a conducted tour.

On the north side of the inner courtyard are the Waterloo Barracks (old weapons and armaments) and the ★ **Jewel House** [O], where the Crown Jewels are kept. Among its treasures are St Edward's Crown, which was made out of pure gold in 1661; the Imperial State Crown with over 3,000 diamonds and other precious stones; the Indian Crown with a 34-carat emerald and over 6,000 diamonds; the Queen Elizabeth Crown with the 108-carat Koh-i-Noor diamond; many other smaller pieces of jewellery, including the royal sceptre with the Star of Africa, cut from the Cullinan diamond and, at 530 carats, the biggest diamond in the world.

A piece of the Crown Jewels

The Regimental Museum [P] and the New Armouries [R] display weapons from the mid-17th to mid-19th century. The Hospital [Q], which dates from the 17th century, is now a residence and may not be visited.

The highlight for many visitors to the Tower of London

New Armouries display

The oldest part of the fortress

St John's Chapel

Towering over London

is the White Tower [S], the oldest part of the fortress. It is 100 ft (30m) tall, the walls are 15ft (5m) thick in places and the four corner towers are all different. Enter the White Tower by the staircase. The interior has changed little and it gives some idea of how a Norman fortress was built. The rooms contain a famous collection of old weapons and armaments. The Romanesque St John's Chapel is the oldest preserved church in London and a perfect example of Norman architecture.

In the southwest corner of the White Tower are the 12th-century remains of the Wardrobe Tower [T] and also some parts of Roman city walls probably dating from the 2nd century. In the Bowyer Tower (behind Waterloo Barracks) are weapons of torture and execution.

Tower Bridge 67. Built at the end of the 19th century, its two 200-ft (66-m) high towers have come to symbolise London. (It is often mistakenly taken to be 'London Bridge' by visitors from abroad.) Each section of the bridge weighs 1,100 tons and when closed carries Tower Bridge Road traffic. It takes 90 seconds for the bascules to open fully for large ships to pass under. The Tower Bridge walkway which links the towers gives a good view of the Thames. Reopened in autumn 1993, the London Bridge Experience Museum illustrates the history of the bridge and how the mechanism works, and provides a fascinating glimpse into the Victorian era (walkway and museum 10am–6.30pm, in winter 10am–4.45pm).

West of Tower Bridge and reached from the south bank is the World War II cruiser *HMS Belfast* 68 (10am–5.20pm, in winter 10am–4pm). In the **St Katharine's Dock** 69 boating marina are the famous Dickens Inn pub and the round Coronarium Chapel, built in 1977 to celebrate Elizabeth II's silver jubilee. There is also a historic ship collection.

Route 4

Old Bailey – ★★ St Bartholomew the Great – The Barbican – ★★ Museum of London – London Wall – ★Guildhall – St Mary-le-Bow

This route begins at St Paul's Underground station on the north side of the cathedral (*see page 26*). Fork left into Newgate Street and on the right-hand side is the **General Post Office**  and the National Postal Museum on the western side of the King Edward building. It stands on the site of a 14th-century Franciscan monastery. A bastion from the Roman walls can be seen under a loading bay. The Postal Museum houses a unique collection of stamps, documents and books on philately.

The Old Bailey

At the junction of Newgate Street and Old Bailey, turn left for the **Central Criminal Court** ❼, the highest court for criminal cases and usually referred to as the Old Bailey. Its 200-ft (65-m) high dome is crowned with a large bronze statue representing the Lady of Justice. Until 1902, Newgate Prison, London's main prison, stood on this site and until 1868 public executions were carried out in front of it. In 1966, when the courts were being extended, some remains of the city wall dating from Roman and medieval times were discovered.

33

Follow Old Bailey north into Giltspur Street and on the left stands the church of the **Holy Sepulchre** ❼, whose medieval tower and fan vault are preserved. On the right stands **St Bartholomew's Hospital** ❼, which is the oldest hospital in London. Founded in 1123, the present building dates from the 17th and 18th centuries. The church of St Bartholomew the Less is of medieval origin, but only the 15th-century tower is original; it was restored in 1823 and again in 1850. Recent government plans to reorganise London's health service may result in the closure of this venerable institution.

Smithfield Market

West Smithfield ❼ used to be a jousting field and from 1150 to 1855 it served as London's main horse and cattle market and place of execution. Until 1840, one of London's biggest fairs, St Bartholomew's Fair, was also held there. **Smithfield Market** ❼, an unlikely confection of iron and plaster, is still the biggest meat market in Britain. The best time to visit it is Monday to Wednesday between 9–11am.

One of London's finest sights is ★★ **St Bartholomew the Great** ❼ (nearest Underground station: *Barbican*), situated to the east of West Smithfield. It is the oldest of London's churches, after St John's Chapel in the Tower.

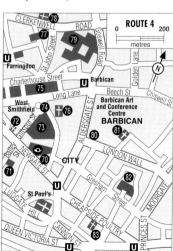

St Bartholomew the Great

Great expectations

The Barbican

Built in 1123, the Norman choir with massive round arches is a splendid sight. The transept was added at the end of the 12th century and the Early English-style exterior was completed around 1300.

After the dissolution of the monasteries the church fell into disrepair and by the 18th century it had lost its roof. It was used as a barn, a smithy, a tavern, a warehouse and stables, and it was not until 1929 that a massive rebuilding programme started. The surviving medieval remains have been incorporated into the new structure, so that St Bartholomew's is now one of the finest examples of Norman architecture in Britain.

Rahere (1143), the founder of the church, lies on a decorated tomb beneath a crested canopy. The statue dates from the 12th century, the canopy and wall covering from the 15th century. The Norman gateway leads into the cloister, constructed in 1405 and faithfully restored in 1928. The tower is 17th-century, but the porch dates from the first half of the 13th century.

To the north of Smithfield Market stands **St John's Gate ⓗ** (nearest Underground station: *Farringdon*) and this is the only surviving part of the 11th-century priory belonging to the Order of St John, whose original function was to look after pilgrims visiting the Holy Land. A little further to the north is **St John's ❽**, which was built in 1721 on the site of the old priory. Destroyed during World War II, it has been fully restored. The crypt is the only original priory building to survive.

On the site of the **Medical College ⓦ** was the Charterhouse monastery, which later became a hospital for the destitute.

We now come to **The Barbican**. The futuristic Barbican complex is sometimes described as a 'city within a city', comprising residential areas, schools, shops and open spaces. The Barbican Arts Centre, completed in 1982, is now reckoned to be possibly the biggest cultural centre in the world, offering exhibitions, theatres and concerts. The renowned London Symphony Orchestra is based here, and it is the London home of the Royal Shakespeare Company.

Cross Aldersgate Street to ★★ **The Museum of London** ⑩ (nearest Underground stations: *Barbican*, *St Paul's* or *Moorgate*), which houses countless exhibits illustrating the history of the capital from the original settlement to the present-day city (*see page 73*).

Punch and Judy, Museum of London

London Wall follows the line of the city wall. The many excavated outcrops usually have a Roman base with a medieval upper section. In **St Giles's churchyard** ⑪ some more fragments of the wall are visible. The Sunday morning Petticoat Lane market is in nearby Middlesex Street (*see page 86*).

The ★ **Guildhall** ⑫ (nearest Underground stations: *St Paul's* or *Bank*) is open Monday to Saturday 10am–5pm, in summer also Sunday 10am–5pm. It was built at the beginning of the 15th century, and a neo-Gothic facade was added to the south wall. Seriously damaged by bombing during World War II, the building was fully restored in 1954. Parts of the crypt and the Great Hall have been preserved. The latter (150-ft/50-m long and 90-ft/29-m high) is now the venue for many ceremonial occasions, receptions, meetings and banquets, and the Lord Mayor's show, a colourful parade through the city's streets, starts here each November. The names of the 663 Lord Mayors of London are inscribed on the modern windows, on the window-sills are the coats of arms of the Guilds and a cornice bears the banners of the 12 Great Livery Companies. The 10-ft (3-m) tall figures on the west wall guarding the Musicians' gallery represent Gog and Magog. On the south side is a fine window dating from the 15th century. Behind the Guildhall is the City Exhibition Hall.

35

The Great Hall, Guildhall

Follow King Street south to Cheapside, turn right and on the left stands **St Mary-le-Bow** ⑬. Its origins are Norman, but Sir Christopher Wren rebuilt it between 1670 and 1683. It suffered badly during World War II but was eventually fully restored in 1964. The modern font was presented to the church by the people of Germany. Some bricks dating from Roman times can be seen in the carefully restored crypt (1090).

St Mary-le-Bow

The stone arches or bows, as a stonemason would call them, gave the church its name. The famous Bow Bells ring out from the 240-ft (73-m) bell-tower and the sound has come to define the boundaries of the City. It is traditionally laid down that, to qualify as a true Londoner – usually known as a Cockney, a person must have been born within the sound of Bow Bells.

Route 5

The British Museum

★★★ British Museum – University of London – Dickens's House – ★ Gray's Inn – ★ Lincoln's Inn – Sir John Soane's House

From the Tottenham Court Road Underground station at St Giles Circus, the intersection of Oxford Street, Charing Cross Road and Tottenham Court Road (*see map below*), it is only a short walk to the ★★★ **British Museum** ⑧④, certainly the best-known and most interesting of Britain's museums (*see page 72*).

When the museum outgrew its original location in Montague House, a new building was planned, and eventually completed in 1852. The colonnaded facade, Greek-inspired , measures 400ft (123m) end to end.

Changes are likely over the next few years as the British Library is moving out to St Pancras in 1996, making more space available for museum exhibits. A number of collections are temporarily not on view as they are due to be displayed in rooms and galleries which are undergoing renovation. A simple plan of the museum is provided free.The staircase on the left of the main entrance hall leads to the exhibition of books and manuscripts. Straight ahead is the Reading Room which is crowned with a 110-ft (35-m) dome. It is reckoned to contain the biggest collection

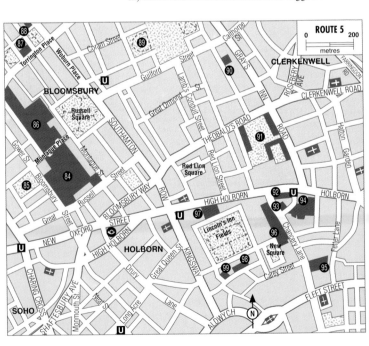

of books in the world with an estimated 18 million volumes on its shelves, and was the daily haunt of many famous writers (including Karl Marx). It can only be used with a special permit.

Biggest collection of books in the world

The highlights of the Greek and Roman antiquities are the Elgin Marbles, friezes and sculptures removed from the Parthenon on the Acropolis in Athens. For many years the Greek government has been asking for their return. They comprise the first interior frieze in Greek history from the Temple of Apollo at Bassae; the Tomb of Mausolus from Halicarnassus and one of the seven wonders of the world; the Caryatid from the Erechtheon on the Acropolis; the monumental statue known as the Strangford Apollo; the famous and elegant Roman hand-blown vase, the Portland Vase.

Marble from the Parthenon

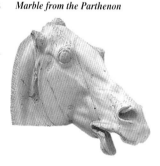

The western Asian exhibits include finds from Nimrud, Nineveh, other Assyrian sites and ancient Palestine. The most important exhibit in the Egyptian gallery is the Rosetta Stone. Written in three languages, Greek, hieroglyphic and demotic scripts, it enabled philologists to unravel the mysteries of hieroglyphics. This gallery also contains a number of animal and human mummies.

The Asian collections include valuable examples of Islamic *objets d'art*, Buddhist antiquities, ancient cloth from central Asia, stone and bronze sculptures from Burma, Indochina, Java and Sri Lanka, and Tibetan Buddhist objects.

In the Indian galleries are some superb stone and bronze sculptures from the 1st century BC. The Japanese and Chinese rooms contain works of art from the earliest years of their cultures and some examples of Korean art.

There are a number of other sections with displays of valuable artefacts from prehistoric times and the European Middle Ages.

In the Manuscript Room are manuscripts of historical and literary significance, Egyptian papyri, Greek, Roman and old English manuscripts and letters from writers, musicians, artists and other historical figures.

The Grenville Library houses some of the most valuable documents, including the oldest Greek Bible, the 4th-century Codex Sinaiticus, the 5th-century Codex Alexandrinus and the original Magna Carta.

Leave the British Museum via the north exit in Montague Place. On the left is **Bedford Square** ㉟, which was laid out in 1775 by the Adam brothers. Robert and James made a great impact on British architecture in the late 18th century and this square with its old town houses is a fine example of their unique style.

North of the British Museum as far as Euston Road is the **Bloomsbury** ㊱ district, now home to many of London University's administrative and academic blocks. The university library, University College, University Hospital and the Royal Academy for Dramatic Art can all be found within this small area. The district also gave its name to the literary circle known as the Bloomsbury Group, formed by the novelist Virginia Woolf. Artists and writers such as Virginia's sister Vanessa, Clive Bell and J M Keynes became associated with the group, which turned its back on traditional Victorian values. The area is blue plaque territory *par excellence*. Virginia Woolf, Roger Fry and Queen Victoria's biographer Lytton Strachey all lived at various addresses around these streets, and their houses are marked with blue plaques.

A little further north is the **Percival David Foundation** ㊲ (nearest Underground station: *Russell Square*) Monday to Friday 10.30am–5pm. This museum of Chinese art was presented to the University of London by Sir Percival David in 1951. Several Chinese dynasties after AD950 are represented in the collections and some of the artefacts belonged to Beijing's imperial collection. The display of Chinese porcelain is particularly interesting.

On the north side of Tavistock Square is the **Jewish Museum** ㊳ (*see page 73*). Its many displays include a valuable collection of Jewish antiquities, writings and prayer books. Head south down Woburn Place and then turn left into Bernard Street to **Coram's Fields** ㊴, the biggest children's playground in London. It is named after Thomas Coram, who in 1745 founded a home for abandoned children on the site. The building was demolished in 1926. On the west side of Coram's Fields, at 40 Brunswick Square, is a small museum which charts the history of Coram's home and also displays an original score of Handel's *Messiah*. Handel had been a supporter of Coram and during his lengthy stay in London directed a choir of children from the house.

Stately Bloomsbury

Exhibit from the Jewish Museum
Coram's Fields

In nearby Doughty Street is **Dickens's House** . The writer lived and worked here from 1837 to 1839. On display in the museum are some of Charles Dickens's letters, first editions, portraits and furniture (Monday to Saturday 10am–5pm). Follow Gray's Inn Road south to ★ **Gray's Inn** (nearest Underground station: *Chancery Lane*), one of the four Inns of Court, the private societies which award barristers' qualifications. This has been a law school since the 14th century. The picturesque buildings with their courtyards and lawns were badly damaged during World War II, but they have all been faithfully restored. In 1594 Shakespeare's *Comedy of Errors* was first performed in the Great Hall, which is also admired for its fine 16th- and 17th-century heraldic windows.

Cross High Holborn to ★ **Staple Inn** , one of the few 16th-century London houses to have survived. Its half-timbered facade, gables and overhanging floors give some idea of how London looked in the days before the Great Fire. Staple Inn was originally the home of wool merchants. Under Henry V it became one of the Inns of Chancery but later amalgamated with Gray's Inn.

Turn into Chancery Lane; on the left are the **London Silver Vaults** .

Here in some 40 rooms, each entered through a strong-room door, silver merchants sell their silver cutlery, tableware and other goods made from this precious metal. The vaults were established in 1882, and many of the items for sale are the original work of modern silversmiths or are reproductions. The dealers also sell jewellery and *objets d'art* made from ivory, enamel and porcelain (*see page 87 for opening times*).

The Patent Office is a few yards to the east .

Further south in Chancery Lane and housed in a neo-Gothic building, which was completed in 1902, is the **Public Records Office** . Important documents from the Middle Ages up to the beginning of the 19th century are stored in this building. The records include Papal Bulls, letters and documents by famous literary and political figures, royal signatures, reports, registers and maps, but they are only available to researchers. There is a small museum adjacent (Monday to Friday 10am–5pm).

Turn right outside the Public Records Office and head back up Chancery Lane to ★ **Lincoln's Inn** (nearest Underground station: *Chancery Lane*), another of the four Inns of Court . Its library, which was founded in 1837, contains about 80,000 legal volumes and is the oldest library in London. The courtyards dating from the 15th century are open to the public. New Square and Old Hall (1491) are worth seeking out for the beautiful 16th- and 17th-century town houses, which now serve as offices for barristers and legal officials. North of the square is the Chapel,

Dickens Display

Lincoln's Inn

An architect's library

Sir John Soane's Museum

A novel expression

originally built in the 1620s in Gothic style, but renovated by Wren in 1685 and enlarged in 1883. The Gatehouse (1518) is accessible from the Old Square and is now remembered as the place where Cromwell lived and studied.

To the north of Lincoln's Inn Fields is **Sir John Soane's Museum ⑨⑦** (nearest Underground station: *Holborn*), which was built by the celebrated architect Sir John Soane in 1812 and was his home until his death. His furnishings and art collections have been left untouched as he stipulated that nothing should be moved or altered and so the displays appear cluttered and untidy (*see also page 75*). The art gallery contains works by Hogarth, Turner and Callcott, the crypt a sarcophagus dating from 1392BC and the New Picture Room works by Watteau and Canaletto. The adjoining houses (Nos 12 and 14) were also built by Soane.

To the south of the square is the Cancer Research Institute and the **Hunterian Museum ⑨⑧**, which belongs to the Royal College of Surgeons and contains one of Europe's most extensive medical collections. It is normally open only to the medical profession.

In the southwest corner of the square, at 13 Portsmouth Street, is the **Old Curiosity Shop ⑨⑨**. Until 1993 lovers of the works of Charles Dickens could visit this antiques shop which, according to the inscription, was the inspiration for his novel *The Old Curiosity Shop*. As we went to press, the building was closed and up for sale.

To return to Tottenham Court Road, follow either the Strand or New Oxford Street or find the nearest Underground stations which are *Aldwych* or *Temple*.

Route 6

London Bridge – ★★ Southwark Cathedral – The Globe – George Inn

At the southern end of London Bridge stands Southwark Cathedral (*see below*) but the best place to start this route is at the northern end of the bridge. From Monument Underground station walk towards the bank of the river and the **Fishmongers' Hall** ⓿. The fishmongers' guild established their hall here in 1504, but after the Great Fire it was rebuilt and in the 1830s a new facade was added.

Cross the Thames via **London Bridge** ⓵ . The new bridge was opened in 1973, but a bridge of some kind has stood on the site since Saxon times. The only bridge over the Thames until 1749 was made of stone at the beginning of the 13th century. Finally rebuilt in 1832, it was dismantled in 1968 and is now in Arizona. On the south side of London Bridge stands the post-modern London Bridge City office and shopping centre.

London Bridge Station ⓶ was the first station to be opened in London and it now serves commuters from the southern suburbs of London. In Tooley Street are the London Dungeons ⓷ (*see page 73*).

You can't miss ★★ **Southwark Cathedral** ⓸ (nearest Underground station: *London Bridge*).

Southwark Cathedral

It stands on the site of a Saxon church said to have been built around 666. In 1106 it was modified in Norman style, but after a fire in 1206 it was completely rebuilt as the first of London's Gothic-style churches. The base of the 160-ft (54-m) tower remains, as do the choir, chancel aisle and pillars at the centre of the transept. The nave dates from the 13th century but it was altered in 1469 and was not restored to its original style until the end of the 19th century.

Enter the cathedral at the southwest entrance [A] and on the left, behind the font, the remains of the 13th-century Gothic arcading [B] are clearly visible. In the northwest corner are wooden ceiling bosses [C] rescued from the 15th-century wooden roof. There are fragments of a 12th-century Norman arch [D] in the north wall which originally led into the cloisters of the old monastery. The tomb of John Gower [E] (1408), a poet and friend of Chaucer, is to be found in the north aisle, while opposite in the south aisle is a 1912 alabaster monument to William Shakespeare [F]. This stands below the Shakespeare Memorial window (1954), which displays characters from the bard's plays.

41

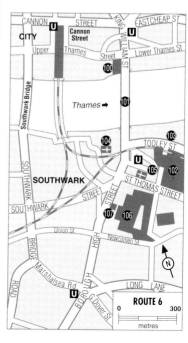

*London's first
Gothic-style church*

The central tower is supported by four huge pillars and a richly decorated oak Jacobean chair [G] can be seen at the foot of the southwest pillar. The south transept [H] dates from 1310 and standing on the west wall are a bust of Chancellor of the Exchequer Frederick Wigan and a monument (1614) to the President of the Church Council and royal saddler, John Bingham. On the east wall, close to the southern entrance [I], hang the red painted arms and hat of Cardinal Beaufort (1447).

The wall arches in the north transept [J] are well maintained and the tombstones date from the beginning of the 18th century. The Harvard Chapel [K] lies to the east of the north transept and it takes its name from John Harvard who founded the eponymous American university. He was baptised here in 1607.

The north chancel aisle is reached by passing under an elegant stilted arch and on the wall stands a colourful monument to John Trehearne [L], with his wife and six children dressed in costumes of the period (1618). Beyond are the figure of a knight [M], possibly a Templar, from the 13th century and the monument to Richard Humble [N] and his wives in full 17th-century finery. In the south chancel aisle lie the 17th-century tombs of bishops Lancelot Andrews [O] and Edward Talbot [P].

The choir [Q] was built in 1273 and to the north of the sanctuary the bishops' seats [R] are particularly interesting. The altar [S] in Perpendicular style dates from 1520, although the pillars are 13th century.

The 13th-century retrochoir [T] has been restored on a number of occasions. On the north side is a 16th-century oak chest with some delicate marquetry and to one side is a model of a 17th-century Dutch sailing ship. Of the four chapels at the eastern end of the cathedral, the 1228 Chapel of the Virgin Mary [U] is remarkable for its true Early English style.

To the north of the cathedral, the Nancy Steps, which featured in Charles Dickens's *Oliver Twist*, lead on to London Bridge.

Twisted steps

During the 16th and 17th centuries the area to the west of the cathedral, dominated today by warehouses and a disused power station, used to be the entertainment centre for London. The Hope Theatre, the Rose Theatre and, most famous of all, the Globe Theatre, where Shakespeare sometimes appeared in his own plays, were all situated here. **The Globe** is presently being reconstructed and is due to open in the summer of 1995.

In St Thomas Street stands the church of **St Thomas** **105** . Dating from the beginning of the 18th century, it is now the chapter house for Southwark Cathedral and it is well worth a visit. At one time a hospital stood on this site and the semi-circular 'operating theatre' has been preserved in its original state and may be visited (Tuesday to Sunday 10am–4pm; closed from mid-December until the beginning of January). The nearby **Guy's Hospital** **106** was founded in the 18th century.

43

Since the Middle Ages, Borough High Street has been one of the main roads out of London towards the south coast and it has many historical landmarks. One such is the **George Inn** **107** at number 77, a 17th-century tavern and formerly a coaching house, which Dickens immortalised in *Little Dorrit*. It is the last of the many galleried inns that once lined this road; scrubbed wood, blackened paint, open hearth and galleried courtyard evoke the London of the 1670s.

The sign of good ale

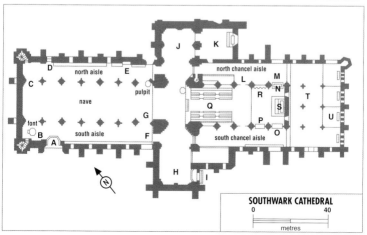

SOUTHWARK CATHEDRAL
0   40
metres

Route 7

Waterloo Station – ★ Royal Festival Hall – ★★ Hayward Gallery – Royal National Theatre – Old Vic – ★ Imperial War Museum

Waterloo Station

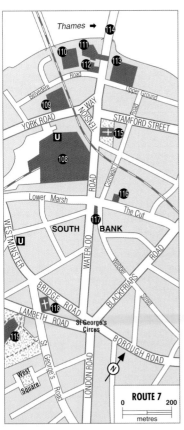

Waterloo Station 108 (nearest Underground station: *Waterloo*) is the main station for southern and southeast England. The present building was constructed between 1912 and 1922 and it has become the biggest station in Britain. The latest addition is the spectacular new terminus housing the long platform for the Channel Tunnel trains, the first of which arrived in 1994.

On the other side of York Road is the 26-storey **Shell Centre** 109. Not only is it the British headquarters of the Shell oil company but it is also a leading training and conference centre.

A little further north by the riverside is the South Bank Arts Centre which comprises a number of interesting buildings. The ★ **Royal Festival Hall** 110 (nearest Underground stations: *Waterloo* or *Charing Cross*, then cross the Hungerford footbridge) is one of Britain's major concert halls. It was opened in 1951 to celebrate the Festival of Britain and it can accommodate 3,000 people. To the north is **Queen Elizabeth Hall** 111, which was opened in 1967. As well as the main hall with seats for 1,100, there is the smaller Purcell Room, the National Film Theatre and the Museum of the Moving Image, which documents the history of cinema and television. In the southeast corner of the complex is the ★★ **Hayward Gallery** 112. Run under the auspices of the Arts Council, there are a total of five galleries in this terrace-like concrete structure dating from the late 1960s. The rooms are all of different dimensions and a complicated lighting system ensures that the intensity of light within the galleries remains the same. The exhibitions of sculptures and paintings are changed regularly, and it is also a venue for temporary international exhibitions and loans from other museums.

On the east side of Waterloo Road, is the impressive **Royal National Theatre** 113. Built in 1976, it comprises three theatres: the Olivier, the Lyttelton and the Cottesloe. The productions range from classical to modern, experimental drama. Waterloo Bridge 114 spans the Thames at this point. On the opposite bank Somerset House (*see page 24*) can be clearly seen.

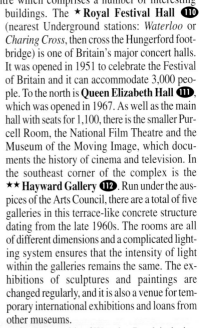

ROUTE 7
0   200
metres

Follow Waterloo Road south and cross Stamford Street. On the left is **St John's** ⑮ , a modern church built for the Festival of Britain in 1951. Continue south under the railway bridge and turn left into The Cut. On the left-hand side is the **Young Vic Theatre** ⑯ . **The Old Vic** ⑰ , for many years the home of the National Theatre Company before it moved a short distance to the new theatre on the South Bank, stands on the corner of The Cut and Waterloo Road. It was threatened with closure but eventually re-opened in 1983 to become a thriving repertory theatre and is currently owned by a Toronto-based retailer, 'Honest Ed' Mervish, and his son.

Continue southwards along Waterloo Road and at St George's Circus turn right into Lambeth Road. On the right stands **St George's Cathedral** ⑱ , which was one of the first Roman Catholic churches to be built after the Reformation. It was opened in 1848, badly damaged in World War II, and not finally rebuilt until 1963.

Detail of St George's Cathedral

Only a few yards further on, in the garden of the former Bethlehem Hospital, is the ★ **Imperial War Museum** ⑲ (nearest Underground station: *Lambeth North*). Established in 1920, the museum moved to this site in 1936. It was extended and completely redesigned in 1989 and is now equipped with the latest audio-visual displays, making it one of the most modern museums in London. In tune with the times, it is devoted just as much to the frightening experiences that both soldiers and civilians undergo in war as it is to the details of arms and weapons.

45

Though concentrating on World War I and World War II, it covers all the conflicts this century in which Britain has been involved including the Gulf War. In the huge display hall, the highlights are a Polaris rocket, a German V2 rocket, American, British, German and Russian tanks, a German one-man U-boat and a Spitfire, one of many of the aircraft from both world wars which are suspended from the ceiling. The basement displays are concerned with the background, events and effects of the two world wars. Visitors can experience for themselves the 1940 Blitz in a London street or the conditions in the trenches in World War I. Other exhibits include uniforms, models of battlefields, paintings, sculptures and photos. The archives and libraries may be visited only by prior arrangement (*see also page 73*).

The Imperial War Museum

There are many fine houses from the 18th and 19th centuries to be seen on either side of Lambeth Road. At 100 Lambeth Road the notorious Captain Bligh of the *Bounty* was born. At the junction of Kennington Road and Westminster Bridge Road once stood the Baptist Christ Church (1878). After World War II, only the tower was left standing. It was built as a memorial tower for Abraham Lincoln. Nearest Underground station: *Lambeth North*.

Spring in Hyde Park

Route 8

Hyde Park Corner – Wellington Arch – Hyde Park – Marble Arch

Hyde Park Corner 120 (nearest Underground station: *Hyde Park Corner*), at the southeast corner of Hyde Park, is reckoned to be the busiest road junction in London. Piccadilly, Park Lane, Knightsbridge and Grosvenor Place all merge at this point (*see map on pages 50–51*), with some traffic going underground.

Wellington Museum

In the middle of the road on a traffic island stands the **Wellington Arch 121**, a triumphal arch crowned with a quadriga and a symbolic figure of peace, which was built in 1828. A bronze equestrian statue of Wellington is located in front of Apsley House (*see below*). To the south is the Royal Artillery War Memorial (1928) and to the east the Machine Gun Corps Memorial (1927) with a statue of King David leaning on Goliath's sword.

On the north side of the square is ★ **Apsley House** which houses the **Wellington Museum 122** (*see also page 75*). The residence of the Duke of Wellington (1769–1852) was opened as a museum in 1952 and houses, among many other things, silverplate, Meissen and Sèvres porcelain, batons, swords, and paintings by British and Continental masters including Reynolds, Rubens, Murillo, Velázquez, Goya, Ribera, Guercino and Sassoferato. Most of these were confiscated by Wellington after the Battle of Vitoria in 1813.

Originally designed by Robert Adam for Baron Apsley in 1817, a Corinthian portico and a west wing with the 90-

ft (30-m) Waterloo gallery were added in 1829. It is in the Waterloo gallery where the finest paintings are hung. In the staircase vestibule stands a Carrara marble sculpture of Napoleon by Canova.

Behind Apsley House is the entrance to **Hyde Park**. When combined with Kensington Gardens, this famous green space constitutes the biggest public park in London. It was once owned by Westminster Abbey, but Henry VIII closed off the area and the park was stocked with deer and kept as a royal chase. Charles I opened it up to the people in 1635. A tripartite screen designed by Decimus Burton and erected in 1828 marks the entrance to the park and the reliefs above the middle arch are copies of the Parthenon frieze which can be seen in the British Museum (*see pages 36–37*).

For the birds

There are many paths across the park: the South Carriage Drive follows the southern edge of the park from the entrance as far as Alexandra Gate; another path heads north alongside Park Lane to the northeast entrance by Marble Arch. More or less parallel to South Carriage Drive is the horse promenade, Rotten Row or *route du roi* (the king's path), which was once taken by the king on his way to the royal hunting grounds and is still used by well-heeled riders and their mounts. Just inside the entrance is the **Achilles statue** which was erected in 1822 in honour of the Duke of Wellington.

Follow the middle path northeast to the **Serpentine**, a long, narrow lake which is a haven for wildfowl and a popular spot for boating, swimming and fishing. Caroline von Ansbach, George II's wife, commissioned the excavation of the lake in 1730.

Continue along the north shore of the lake. Shortly before the bridge is Jacob Epstein's *Rima*, a memorial unveiled in 1925 to the American-born British author and naturalist W. H. Hudson. The memorial is set back against trees on the right and has a formal pool in front of it.

Serpentine Bridge detail

The **Serpentine bridge** offers a splendid view over the park and with a restaurant and gallery (*see page 75*) nearby it is a focal point for visitors to the park. Naturalists are often surprised to find that, despite the hustle and bustle of the metropolis, some relatively rare species such as the heron have settled here. The best time to see these fine birds is around daybreak.

To the west of the bridge, the Serpentine is known as the Long Water and on the western side of this arm of the lake is the statue of **Peter Pan**. As well as many other statues, there is a fountain and a pavilion. Whether it is for the long walks, gardens and open spaces or the bandstands, restaurants and art gallery, Hyde Park is an ideal place to relax and a popular haunt for Londoners and visitors alike.

Speakers' Corner

Street art

To leave the park, make for the northeast corner and Speakers' Corner **127**, where the British exercise their right to free speech. This is the location of the ancient Tyburn gallows (*see below*), where the condemned were allowed to speak freely before being executed. This right of free speech was extended to everyone, and today speakers, often assisted by megaphones, are allowed to express whatever views they like (usually political or religious) without fear of repression or censorship. Saturday and Sunday are the best days to listen to the sometimes extreme opinions of the soapbox orators, but the quick-witted audiences can provide good entertainment, with highly experienced hecklers doing their best to challenge any speech with critical and often abusive remarks. It's a good training ground for public speakers.

Bayswater Road borders the north side of the park and on Sundays and Bank Holidays artists display their work on the park railings.

Beyond Speakers' Corner, in the middle of a busy square surrounded by traffic and dominating the busy junction of Oxford Street, Edgware Road, Park Lane and Bayswater Road, is **Marble Arch 128** (nearest Underground station: *Marble Arch*). This huge triumphal arch of Italian marble was designed by John Nash in 1828, but lacks a crowning quadriga or statue. The arch, said to be based on the Arch of Constantine in Rome, was originally planned as the royal entrance to Buckingham Palace, but the architect forgot to measure the width of the carriages and the middle arch was too narrow for them. In 1851 the arch was moved to its present location.

Underneath Marble Arch and alongside Park Lane is a huge car-park with space for 1,000 vehicles. From the 12th century to 1783 the present site of Marble Arch was used for public executions. A stone in the park railings in Bayswater Road marks the spot where the gallows used to stand.

Starting from Marble Arch and running east for 1½ miles (2½km) is Oxford Street, the busiest shopping street in London (*see page 84*).

Park Lane links Marble Arch and Hyde Park Corner. It used to be home for the aristocracy in their expensive town residences, but it is now lined on the east side with luxury hotels including the Dorchester, Grosvenor House and the Hilton.

Further east of Park Lane is the so-called 'American quarter' centred on **Grosvenor Square 129** with the American Embassy, the American Society, General Eisenhower's former headquarters during World War II, and the memorial to the American President Franklin D Roosevelt. The cost of the statue was met by grateful British citizens after World War II.

Route 9

★ Kensington Palace – Albert Memorial – Royal Albert Hall – ★Science Museum – ★Natural History Museum ★★ Victoria and Albert Museum – Harrods

This walk through Kensington Gardens and the museum area can be undertaken as a continuation of the previous route. From either Lancaster Gate or Queensway Underground stations, enter the extensive grounds through Marlborough Gate ⓭⓪, Lancaster Gate ⑬ or Black Lion Gate ⓭②.

Kensington Palace

Kensington Gardens adjoin the west side of Hyde Park and there are some pleasant walks from the gates along the north side of the gardens to ★ **Kensington Palace** ⓭③ (nearest Underground station: *Queensway*) Monday to Saturday 9.30am–5pm, Sunday 11am–5.30pm. The palace, the work of Sir Christopher Wren and William Kent, was the residence of the kings and queens of England from 1689 to 1760. The state apartments on the first floor, decorated in the early Georgian and Victorian styles, were first opened to the public in 1956. Many of the other rooms are now the residences of members of the royal family and the aristocracy. On display are art treasures (paintings, china, silver and various antiques) from the collections of Queen Mary and Queen Victoria, who were both born in the palace.

Antiques galore
Kensington Gardens

In front of the palace is the Round Pond, a favourite haunt of model-boat enthusiasts. Only a few yards from the palace, but just outside the park, is **Kensington Church Street** ⓭④ with its many antique shops. To the south is Kensington High Street, a busy shopping street

(*see page 25*; nearest Underground station: *High Street Kensington*), which leads to the **Commonwealth Institute** ㉟. This impressive modern building, opened in 1962, houses several famous collections which give some insight into the life, culture, scenery and natural resources of the Commonwealth countries. An art centre and gallery (*see page 72*) is adjacent.

To the north is Holland Park, with its splendid rose beds, peacocks and the Holland Court Theatre. Parts of Holland House, the 17th-century mansion, remain.

On the edge of Kensington Gardens stands the **Albert Memorial** ⑬, Sir Gilbert Scott's national monument to the Prince Consort, Prince Albert of Saxe-Coburg Gotha (1819–61). Work on the 175-ft (60-m) high memorial began in 1863, and was completed 13 years later. The seated figure of Prince Albert, itself 15ft (5m) in height, is protected by a Gothic canopy. Depicted in marble relief at the base are 178 figures from the world of art and science. The marble figures on the lower corners of the steps symbolise America, Asia, Africa and Europe while those above represent agriculture, industry, trade and architecture. Renovation work on the memorial, under wraps since 1992, has begun. The **Royal Albert Hall** ⑬ stands on the other

Royal Albert Hall

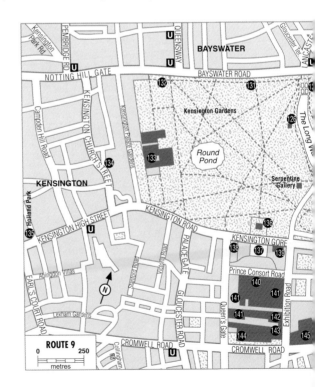

side of Kensington Gore. Built between 1867 and 1871, the concert hall has seats for 8,000 people. Shaped like a great amphitheatre beneath a huge glass dome, the hall is used mainly for rallies, boxing, conferences and concerts, including the Henry Wood Promenade concerts held every summer (*see page 77*).

West of the Albert Hall stands the **Royal College of Art** 🔟. This is an institute for graduate students, but there is also a small gallery, with changing exhibitions open to the public. To the east is the **Royal Geographical Society** 🔟 with its collection of over 500,000 maps, as well as commemorative articles on great explorers, but it is not open to the general public. To the south are the imposing buildings of the **Royal College of Music** 🔟 and the **Imperial College of Science and Technology** 🔟.

The ★ **The Science Museum** 🔟 (*see page 74*), which was built between 1913 and 1928, houses many exhibits demonstrating scientific and technical achievements over the centuries and the application of mathematics, physics and chemistry to the various fields of technology. The displays include a model of the Foucault pendulum which proves the rotation of the earth on its own axis, Stephenson's first steam engines, Alexander Graham Bell's first

*Imperial College
The Science Museum*

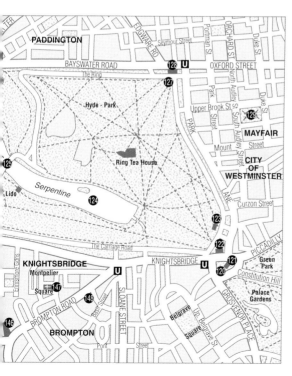

telephone, Murdoch's first gasworks and Galileo's telescopes, as well as the equipment for the generation of the first X-rays, atomic physics equipment, Otto Lilienthal's first-sailplane, models of famous ships, spacecraft and earth satellites. A covered way leads from here to the adjoining **Geological Museum** **143** which is now an integrated part of the ★ **Natural History Museum** **144** occupying the palatial building to the south (nearest Underground station: *South Kensington*).

The museum was built between 1873–80 in neo-Gothic style. The terracotta tiles depicting animals give added interest to the 685-ft (225-m) long facade. The museum is divided into the Life Galleries (natural history section) and the Earth Galleries (geology section).

The Life Galleries are accessible via the main entrance in Cromwell Road. The ground floor is devoted to human biology, ecology, the study of insects as well as the ever-popular dinosaurs. The largest dinosaur skeleton, that of a Diplodocus, is given pride of place in the entrance hall, amongst the Wonders of the Natural History Museum, but the dinosaurs have also been assigned their very own gallery, number 21, where visitors can walk among a whole variety of skeletons and even encounter some flesh-eating robotic species. The first floor is devoted to evolution and mammals, and also contains collections of minerals and meteorites. In the Earth Galleries, the visitor can marvel at the collections of precious and semi-precious stones, learn about the history of the earth and even experience a simulated volcanic eruption.

A hit with the young people is the new Discovery Centre, where 7- to 11-year-olds are invited to explore the natural world. (For opening times *see page 74*.)

The Victoria and Albert Museum

Only a few yards further to the east is the impressive Renaissance facade of the ★★ **Victoria and Albert Museum** **145** (nearest Underground station: *South Kensington, see page 75*).

Built between 1899 and 1909, it is a vast storehouse of decorative arts. The collections originated from purchases of contemporary works displayed at the 1851 Exhibition. Above the impressive main entrance in Cromwell Road stand the statues of Queen Victoria and Prince Albert beside those of King Edward VII and Queen Alexandra. In the niches between the windows of the south and west front are statues of famous artists. The Henry Cole Wing was completed in 1983.

To visit all sections of the museum with its centuries-old treasures from around the world requires more than a day and it is a good idea to buy a catalogue. The museum houses some impressive collections of sculpture, pottery and china, engravings and illustrations, metalwork, paintings, including several works by John Constable, textiles and period costumes from many countries, and wood carvings, including medieval religious works. In the section devoted to furniture design, the rooms are furnished entirely in the style of their period. There are also sections on the Far East, India and Southern Asia and a large art library.

Just east of the museum is the **Brompton Oratory**  the Roman Catholic church of a priestly order founded in Rome by St Philip Neri. The church, with its 190-ft (66-m) dome, was built between 1854 and 1884 in the Italian baroque style and contains great Carrara marble statues of the apostles, which once graced the cathedral at Siena. Also noteworthy are the mosaics of the saints on the cornices above the arches to the side chapels, the 1693 altar leaf of the Lady Chapel, which was brought from the Dominican church at Brescia, and the altar leaf from St Wilfred's Chapel in Maastricht Cathedral (1710).

Only a few hundred yards away in Montpelier Square stands the **German Evangelical Church of Christ** ❼ It can be reached either by the nearest Underground station, South Kensington, or by following Brompton Road in a northeasterly direction.

Near Brompton Road is **Harrods** ❽, the most famous department store in London and patronised by the royal family (*see page 85*). The elegant food hall is decorated with art nouveau tiles and mosaics. The store was started by Henry Charles Harrod when his grocery business opened in 1849, although the present building was opened in 1905. The business is now owned by the Egyptian Al-Fayed family, who purchased this and other House of Fraser outlets for £615 million in 1983.

Inside the Brompton Oratory

Route 10

Regent Street – Soho – Oxford Street – Portland Place – ★ Madame Tussaud's – ★ Regent's Park

This route begins in Regent Street (*see page 84*) and leads through **Soho**, the heart of London's nightlife with its dozens of nightclubs, cabarets and strip clubs. By day the area's cosmopolitan atmosphere is more obvious. Chinese, Indian, Arabic, Spanish and Italian restaurants abound and the streets throng with people from all over the world. Having acquired a reputation for sleaziness, the area was cleaned up in the 1980s but has recently been sliding downhill again. In the 1960s the now legendary **Carnaby Street** ④⑨ became the focal point for a popular youth culture. It now lives on its reputation and has become a tourist attraction in its own right.

Carnaby Street cutie

Golden Square ⑮⓪ grew up as the centre of London's wool trade in the 17th century but much of the media industry is now based there. The statue in the centre of the square shows George II in Roman costume.

At the end of Broadwick Street is **Berwick Street market** ⑮①, a typical Soho market with a reputation for selling the cheapest fruit and vegetables in London. It is surrounded by discotheques and strip clubs and leads into Wardour Street, the centre of the British film industry. At the end of Wardour Street is Old Compton Street, a typical Soho thoroughfare with a wide choice of foreign restaurants and food stores.

54   *Berwick Street Market*

The church of **St Anne's Soho** ⑮② is also situated here, and its tower bears memorial plaques to the writer William Hazlitt, who is buried here, and King Theodore of Corsica who died in Soho in 1756.

On the left a few yards further on is 28 Dean Street, where Karl Marx lived with his family between 1851 and 1856. It was during this time that he wrote his great work *Das Kapital* in the Reading Room at the British Museum library. He was also buried in London, at Highgate cemetery, where his tomb has become a place of pilgrimage.

Soho Square ⑮③ (nearest Underground station: *Tottenham Court Road*) was one of London's most refined squares in the 18th century but only numbers 36 on the west side and 21A on the east side survive from that time. On the north side is the French Protestant Church, completed in 1893, and on the east side the Roman Catholic church of St Patrick, built at around the same time. On the southeast corner of the square stands St Barnabas House for the poor and homeless, noted for its rococo stucco work and entrance steps. The monument to Charles II in the centre of the square dates from the 18th century. Greek Street, which leads off Soho Square, is another street noted for its fine restaurants. At the north end of Greek Street is Oxford Street, London's busiest shopping street (*see page 84*).

At Oxford Circus underground station turn right into Regent Street to arrive, via Cavendish Square and Langham Place, at **Portland Place**. This boulevard, laid out in 1774 by the Adam brothers, is one of Britain's widest streets. The BBC's Broadcasting House, many foreign embassies and several scientific institutes are located here. Towering above the city, at the end of New Cavendish Street, is the **British Telecom Tower** ● (nearest Underground stations: *Goodge Street, Warren Street* or *Great Portland Street*), Britain's second tallest building (580ft/180m or 680ft/200m including antenna). This tower, also known by its old name, Post Office Tower, was built in 1965 as a receiving and transmitter station. At the time, a major attraction was its revolving restaurant, the first of its kind in the country, but both this and the viewing platforms have long been closed for security reasons.

At the northern end of Portland Place is Park Square. The semi-circular **Park Crescent** ● (nearest Underground station: *Regent's Park*), distinguished by the elegant town houses with Ionic colonnades, was built in 1821 by John Nash. On the east side is the modern International Student House built in 1965 with a bust of John F Kennedy outside.

Just a short walk to the north is the southeast entrance to Regent's Park. Before visiting the park it is worth following Marylebone Road a few yards to the right where the road leads past the Royal Academy of Music to ★ **Madame Tussaud's Wax Museum** ● (nearest Underground station: *Baker Street*. Daily 10am–5.30pm). This is a very popular attraction but, by buying tickets in advance at a travel agent, it is possible to avoid the long queues. The museum, founded by the Swiss Madame Tussaud in 1776, moved several times before becoming established in its present-day home in 1884. It houses the oldest and largest collection of wax effigies of the famous and infamous, past

Hot wax and the Fab Four

Regent's Park boating lake

Regent's Park Canal

and present. The Chamber of Horrors displays gruesome scenes of terror including a wax tableau of the Battle of Trafalgar.

The **Planetarium** 157, adjacent to Madame Tussaud's, opened in 1958 and was Britain's first planetarium. The internal surface of the cupola is used as a projection screen for guided tours of the stars and planets. (Demonstrations take place Monday to Sunday 12.20–5pm.)

Nearby **Baker Street Station** 158 is worth a visit. Baker Street is London's oldest surviving Underground station. The first Tube service to Waterloo Station started from here in 1906. From here it is just a short walk to ★ **Regent's Park** 159 (nearest Underground stations: *Baker Street* or *Regent's Park*). This former royal hunting ground was remodelled as a park between 1812 and 1827 by John Nash, who was also responsible for the magnificent terraces of nearby houses built in the Classical style. The park has a large boating lake, tennis courts and other sports facilities, fine walks in and around the Queen Mary's Rose Garden and an open-air theatre, where Shakespeare's plays are performed in summer.

Pleasure boats cruise along the Regent's Park Canal, an extension of the Grand Union Canal, which borders the north side of the park. ★★ **London Zoo** 160 is also situated to the north of the park (daily 9am–6pm, Sunday until 7pm, in winter 10am–dusk). Home to some 12,000 animals, it is one of the world's oldest zoos, whose primary function lies in research and preservation. A varying programme enables visitors to make closer acquaintance with individual animals; children especially will enjoy feeding the animals and riding the camels.

On the way back to Oxford Street via Baker Street or Marylebone High Street, it is worth also trying to fit in a visit to the famous ★ **Wallace Collection** (*see page 75*).

Route 11

Victoria Station – ★ Westminster Cathedral – Victoria Tower Gardens – ★ Lambeth Palace – ★★ Tate Gallery

This walk begins at **Victoria Station** ⓫ (nearest Underground station: *Victoria*), the main station of departure for trains to southern England and Gatwick airport. There is also a London Tourist Board information office (*see page 99*) and a hotel accommodation service. The **Green Line Coach Station** ⓬ and **Victoria Coach Station** ⓭ are both nearby.

Buckingham Palace Road runs alongside the station to Buckingham Palace (*see page 22*) and also to the **Royal Mews** ⓮, end of March–end of September, Tuesday to Thursday noon–4pm; beginning of October–end of March, Wednesday noon–4pm. Here horsedrawn coaches and carriages used by the Royal Family for official occasions are on display. There is the Gold State Coach built in 1762 for George III, the Wedding Coach and the Coronation Coach, as well as a number of fine Rolls Royce cars. The finely groomed horses are also a great attraction.

Near the station at the lower end of Victoria Street is a busy shopping precinct. A short walk across Ashley Place is ★ **Westminster Cathedral** ⓯, Britain's main Roman Catholic church and the seat of the Archbishop of Westminster. The Byzantine-style red brick cathedral was built between 1895 and 1903. It is 390ft (120m) long and 170ft (52m) wide and its bell tower, served by a lift to the viewing gallery, is 310ft (95m) high. The inside

57

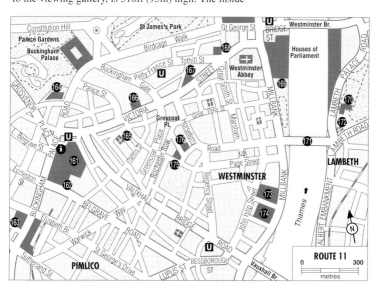

Westminster Cathedral

of the cathedral is superbly decorated with marble and mosaics. Enter through the portico and immediately on the left is a bronze of St Peter, which is a copy of the one in St Peter's in Rome. To the right of the high altar is the Lady Chapel and from here stairs lead down to the crypt, where ancient relics are stored. A guide to the church is available at the entrance.

In Victoria Street there are several notable modern buildings, such as ★**Westminster City Hall** **166** built in 1966, and **New Scotland Yard** **167** , the headquarters of the Metropolitan Police, which was built in 1968. On the corner of Tothill Street is **Methodist Central Hall** **168** and the new building next to it is the Queen Elizabeth II Conference Centre. Westminster Abbey is situated opposite (*see pages 19–21*).

Victoria Tower Gardens **169** lie beside the Thames (nearest Underground station: *Westminster*). The gardens, from which there is a fine view across the river, contain memorials to Emmeline Pankhurst and her daughter, who were instrumental in winning votes for women. A bronze copy of Rodin's *Burghers of Calais* is also worth a look.

On the opposite side of the Thames is ★**Lambeth Palace** **170** which has been the Archbishop of Canterbury's London residence for 800 years. Despite many alterations, the 12th-century palace buildings have retained their medieval appearance. The Archbishop's apartments are in the north wing of the palace, which was built in the neo-Gothic style between 1828 and 1833. A part of the park is accessible to the public.

Also on this side of the river is St Thomas's Hospital with the Florence Nightingale Museum (*see page 72*).

The stylised pineapples on either end of **Lambeth Bridge**  are a memorial to botanist John Tradescant, horticulturalist to Charles II, who was the first to cultivate pineapples successfully in England. He lies buried in the graveyard of the church of **St Mary at Lambeth** next door to the palace, which is now home to the Museum of Garden History (March–December, Monday to Friday 11am–3pm, Sunday 10.30am–5pm). The grave of Admiral Bligh of the *Bounty* can also be found in this idyllic cemetery.

Detail of St Mary's

Millbank leads along the bank of the Thames, past the 420-ft (130-m) Millbank Tower office block (once heralded as the tallest building in London, but now much overshadowed) and **Queen Alexandra's Military Hospital** to the ★★ **Tate Gallery** (nearest Underground station: *Pimlico*).

The Tate Gallery

This important gallery, built on the site of the Millbank penitentiary, was opened in 1897 and was extended in 1910, 1926 and 1937. It houses a collection of paintings and modern sculpture which grew from a gift by the wealthy collector Sir Henry Tate. There is a particularly rich collection of English art from the 16th century to the present day, including work by Kneller, Lely, Gainsborough, Hogarth, Reynolds, Wilson, Constable, Turner and Blake. An extensive collection of French Impressionists includes work by Cézanne, Degas, Gauguin, Manet, Monet, Pissarro, Utrillo, Rousseau and Bonnard. Paintings by Braque, Chagall, Munch, Picasso, Klee, Kokoschka, Dufy, Gris, Léger, Matisse, Vlaminck and many other 20th-century artists can also be seen here. Among the collection of sculptures are pieces by Arp, Rodin, Giacometti, Marini, Manzù, Epstein and Moore.

Because of its richness and variety, only about one sixth of the collection can be shown at any one time, so exhibits are changed quite frequently. The Tate's own catalogues, available from the entrance hall, are very useful guides to the gallery.

The artist JMW Turner bequeathed a vast amount of works to the nation (about 300 paintings and over 19,000 drawings and watercolours). Although he died in 1851, it was not until 1987 that the Clore Gallery, built onto the side of the Tate, was eventually opened to house the entire **Turner Collection**.

Between Westminster Cathedral (*see page 57*) and the Tate Gallery are the **Old Horticultural Hall** and the **New Horticultural Hall** , both centres for exhibitions and flower shows. Narcissi are exhibited in April, rhododendrons in May, irises in June, and roses in July and September. In July, August and September there are shows of carnations, gladioli, dahlias and chrysanthemums which last until November.

Route 12

Sloane Square – Battersea Park – King's Road

This walk through the fashionable district of Chelsea begins at **Sloane Square** 🔢 (nearest Underground station: *Sloane Square*), whose centrepiece is an attractive fountain by Gilbert Ledward (1953). The east side of the square is occupied by the Royal Court Theatre where early works by George Bernard Shaw were performed between 1904 and 1907 and which maintains a high reputation today.

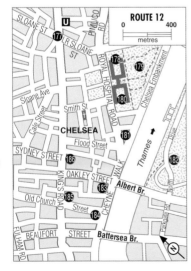

Follow Lower Sloane Street to the **Chelsea Hospital** 🔢 (Monday to Saturday 10am–12 noon, 2–4pm, in summer Sunday 2–4pm). This hospital and home for war veterans was built by Sir Christopher Wren between 1682–92. The Great Hall features a display of royal portraits and captured flags and standards. The east wing houses a museum tracing the history of the hospital. The Figure Court contains a fine bronze statue of Charles II.

Chelsea Hospital

Ranelagh Gardens 🔢, which borders the hospital to the south, is a popular place for a stroll by the Thames. A few yards away is the **National Army Museum** 🔢 (*see page 74*), and just beyond is the **Chelsea Physic Garden** 🔢 with a memorial to the scientist Sir Hans Sloane.

On the opposite bank of the Thames is the extensive **Battersea Park** 🔢. It contains sculptures by Henry Moore, a children's zoo, a lake and exotic plants.

Battersea's peace pagoda

Follow Cheyne Walk with its attractive 18th- and 19th-century houses and turn right into Cheyne Row, where a memorial to Thomas Carlyle marks **Carlyle's House** 🔢 The historian lived here between 1834–81. The house contains mementoes of Carlyle, author of *The French Revolution*. A short walk to the west leads to **Chelsea Old Church** 🔢, built in the 12th century and restored most recently in 1958. It houses several remarkable memorials and monumental tombs. At the end of Old Church Street is the junction with King's Road. Here, the popular **Chelsea Antique Market** 🔢 is a good place to browse and perhaps pick up a real bargain.

King's Road (*see page 85*) is not only a busy shopping street but also the centre for London's artists. Smart bistros, cafés, restaurants and boutiques characterise this very fashionable and expensive part of London. At the top of Sydney Street is **Chelsea Town Hall** 🔢, dating from 1887. In spring and autumn, its art auctions only offer lots which predate 1830. These auctions enjoy a reputation which extends far beyond the shores of Great Britain.

Route 13

Westminster Bridge – Victoria Embankment – Cleopatra's Needle – Her Majesty's Ships

This walk along the Victoria Embankment begins at **Westminster Bridge** ⑱⑦ (nearest Underground station: *Westminster*). The bridge is 886ft (270m) long and was built between 1854 and 1862. A large bronze statue dating from 1902 shows Queen Boadicea on her chariot (*see page 9*). The pier for Thames cruises is by the bridge and from this point there is a fine view of **County Hall** ⑱⑧ on the opposite bank. Built between 1912 and 1933, it was the seat of the Greater London Council until 1986. It has several interesting features, including an unusually steep roof and a colonnaded arc in the middle of the 820-ft (250-m) Thames facade.

Follow the embankment past several government buildings and the Ministry of Defence's Queen Mary's Terrace, where the **Royal Air Force memorial** ⑱⑨ stands, as far as Charing Cross railway bridge and Hungerford footbridge. Charing Cross Pier is another stop for river cruisers, and there is also a floating restaurant. A short distance further on are the **Embankment Gardens** ⑲⓪ , where there is a café, a bandstand and also several statues of famous Londoners.

Nearby on the bank of the Thames is the 43-ft (13-m) high obelisk, **Cleopatra's Needle** ⑲①. This 180-ton Egyptian pink granite obelisk has no connection whatsoever with Cleopatra, although its popular name has stuck. It was one of a pair of identical obelisks erected in 1500BC by Thutmosis III at Heliopolis. In 1819 the Egyptian viceroy Mohammed Ali gave one to the British nation and in 1878 it was placed on the Thames embankment. The inscriptions describe the deeds of Thutmosis III and Rameses II. The obelisk which completed the pair stands today in New York's Central Park. The modern buildings of the South Bank Centre can be seen on the opposite bank.

On the left just beyond Waterloo Bridge is Somerset House.

Three famous ships are moored on the embankment ⑲②. *HMS Wellington* has become the headquarters of the City's newest guild, the Honourable Company of Master Mariners. *HMS Chrysanthemum* is a Royal Naval Volunteer Reserve training ship and *HMS President* serves as headquarters for the same organisation. Her Majesty's Ships are not accessible to the public.

61

Cleopatra's Needle

Five excursions

1. Docklands and Greenwich

On the south bank of the Thames, about 5 miles (8km) below London Bridge, lies Greenwich, probably the most interesting of the London suburbs.

The best route to Greenwich is to take the fully auto-

Docklands Light Railway

mated **Docklands Light Railway**, which opened in 1987 (Monday to Friday 5.30am–9.30pm or weekend bus service). It runs from Bank or Tower Gateway to the Isle of Dogs, whose southern tip connects with Greenwich via a foot tunnel. Another way to make the return journey is on a Thames cruiser to the Tower or Westminster Pier. This gives a second perspective on the progress of Europe's biggest building project, the transformation of London's Docklands. The old docks area, once so busy but recently so run down, is becoming a new, ultramodern district with office blocks, printing works, housing, shopping centres and its own City Airport. The blend of old, refurbished industrial architecture with a post-modern style is attractive and imposing, but at the same time has provoked great criticism. Visitors can obtain information about the Docklands from the Docklands Visitors Centre, Limeharbour, Isle of Dogs. Monday to Friday 9am–6pm, Saturday and Sunday 10am–4.30pm; guided tours on Tuesday, Thursday and Sunday, tel: 0171-512 1111.

The Cutty Sark

At Greenwich Pier, the arrival and departure point for Thames cruisers, the *Cutty Sark* rests in dry dock. It is the last and one of the most famous English sailing ships that plied the London-East Asia tea route in the 19th century. Built in 1869 the *Cutty Sark* was one of the most graceful and, with a maximum speed of 17 knots, one of the fastest clippers of its time. Below decks is an interesting collection of ship figureheads, drawings and mementoes of voyages to India, Ceylon and China. (Monday to Saturday 10am–6pm, Sunday 12 noon–6pm; in winter until 5pm.) Nearby is *Gipsy Moth IV* in which Sir Francis Chichester made his historic single-handed voyage round the world in 1966–7.

View of the Maritime Museum from the Observatory

Not far from here is the National Maritime Museum, which documents British maritime history through boats, uniforms, etc. (Monday to Saturday 10am–6pm, Sunday 2–5.30pm; in winter until 5pm.) The nearby **Queen's House**, a Palladian villa built by Inigo Jones between 1617 and 1635 is also worth a visit. The Royal Naval College is adjacent and most of this magnificent palace-like building was designed by Sir Christopher Wren. One impressive aspect of the King William building in the southwest is the **Painted Hall**, which dates from 1703 and is decked with portraits by Sir James Thornhill. To the southeast, the chapel in the Queen Mary building was planned by Wren and its altarpiece, *The Shipwreck of Saint Paul*, standing over 25ft (8m) high, is by Benjamin West.

Behind the Royal Naval College lies Greenwich Park, which was laid out by King Louis XIV's gardener Le Nôtre for Charles II. It is home to the former **Observatory** through which runs the Greenwich Meridian, dividing the globe into east and west.

Greenwich Mean Time

About 2½ miles (4km) downstream is the **Thames Flood Barrier** whose 10 steel gates can seal off the Thames within 30 minutes, in the event of a flood warning (Visitors Centre open Monday to Friday 10.30am–5pm, Saturday and Sunday 10.30am–5.30pm). Boat trips leave from Greenwich Pier.

2. Kew Gardens

This pleasant western suburb of London can be reached by the Underground (nearest Underground station: *Kew Gardens* on the District Line). In summer there are daily Thames cruises departing from Westminster Pier.

Kew Gardens (daily 9.30am–dusk), known officially as the Royal Botanic Gardens, extend over 250 acres (100ha), and were laid out in 1759. They are among the world's most beautiful botanical gardens. Visitors can walk for hours along well-tended paths, and over lush lawns, and enjoy superb views of mounds of huge flower beds, shady groups of trees and exotic plants, all with plaques giving both their scientific and common names. Among Kew Gardens' great attractions are two magnificent Victorian greenhouses, built in 1850, whose iron and glass construction was revolutionary, as well as the modern Princess of Wales greenhouse. Other sights include pavilions, a small Greek temple, a Japanese temple gate, a 164-ft (50-m) Chinese pagoda and Kew Palace, built in 1631.

63

Kew: Palace in a garden

3. Richmond

On the right bank of the Thames stands Richmond, the town where once royalty resided, which may be reached by Underground, British Rail or Thames cruiser. The ruins of the original Richmond Palace can still be seen. Built by Edward III, it was rebuilt by Henry VII after its destruction by fire in the 15th century.

The famous view over the Thames from Richmond Hill has been captured by many painters, among them J M W Turner. **Richmond Park** extends over nearly 1500 acres (600ha). In the park are several old houses belonging to aristocratic families, including White Lodge and Pembroke Lodge. Isabella Plantation, a forest reserve and floral paradise dating back to 1831, and the Prince Charles Spinney, with its 5,300 oaks, ashes, beeches, chestnuts and sycamores, are among the jewels in the park's crown.

4. ★★★ Windsor

Visitors to the famous castle on the south bank of the Thames have a choice of either taking a train from Paddington or Waterloo Station, a Green Line bus or an organised tour.

64

Madame Tussaud's heads west

Madame Tussaud's Royalty and Empire wax exhibition opened in 1983 at Windsor's historic railway station. The scene of Queen Victoria's Diamond Jubilee celebrations in 1897 is captured in all its contemporary detail. The railway coach, royal family and guests from all over the world are depicted. (Daily 9.30am–5.30pm, in winter until 4.30pm.)

For nine centuries **Windsor Castle** has served as the royal family's summer residence. The original wooden castle built by William the Conqueror was replaced by a stone building in the mid-13th century. The mighty keep dates from this time, although it received a new facade in 1863. A short time later the Round Tower was built and its 220 steps lead to a terrace with some fine views. In later centuries the castle underwent numerous extensions, alterations and renovations. (It is important to note that much of the castle, including the St George's Hall, was severely damaged by a fire in 1992 and restoration work is still in progress, mainly financed from revenues resulting from the Queen's opening Buckingham Palace to the public during August and September.)

The royals' summer castle

Guided tours would normally lead through the splendidly furnished state apartments with the Great Staircase, Dining Hall, the Queen's Presence Room and other rooms with paintings by great masters such as Rubens and van Dyck. In addition there are the Reception Suite, Picture Gallery and Waterloo Hall, a gallery commemorating the victory over Napoleon. St George's Chapel is worthy of special attention. It was begun in 1477 and is a magnificent example of the Late Gothic Perpendicular style, while also being one of Britain's most beautiful and richly decorated churches. The huge window over the west portal is decorated with 75 painted glass scenes, mostly from the 16th century. The nave, built in 1509, is surprisingly bright. The vaulting is described as a wonder of the builder's art. The choir, from 1484, has oak pews with carved details depicting scenes from the life of St George, Edward III and the Knights of the Order of the Garter.

St George's Chapel

In the choir, Henry VIII, Jane Seymour, Charles I and one of Queen Anne's children are buried. In the crypt below are the tombs of Henry VI, Henry VII, George III, George IV, William IV and George V. The tomb of Edward IV stands to the left of the High Altar. (State Apartments and Chapel open mid-May to mid-October Monday to Saturday 10.30am–5pm, Sunday 1.30–5pm; other times Monday to Saturday 10.30am–3pm.) The State Apartments may not be visited when the Queen is in residence. Because of frequent changes to opening times it is recommended that visitors call the information centre in advance, tel: 0753 831118.

The town of Windsor itself has many delightful timbered houses and inns from the 17th and 18th centuries and is also worth a visit. Visitors can take the bridge across the Thames to **Eton**, famed for its public school that has nurtured many of the nation's leaders.

5. Hampton Court

Hampton Court Palace was built between 1514 and 1525. British Rail serves Hampton Court from Waterloo, and throughout the summer riverboats also run along the Thames from central London.

Henry VIII's home

Under Henry VIII, who took over the building from the disfavoured Cardinal Wolsey, a number of extensions were added to the palace. Its western facade is in typical Tudor red brick. The baroque-style east facade was the work of Sir Christopher Wren. The magnificent Great Hall also originated under Henry VIII. Five of his six wives lived here as queens. The suite of rooms intended for his unfortunate second wife Anne Boleyn was only completed after her execution and subsequently used by Jane Seymour, his third wife, who died giving birth to her son, Edward VI.

It was Queen Victoria who opened the palace to the public. In the Clock Court is an astronomical clock from 1540. The **palace gardens** burst into bloom in mid-May. The biggest garden show in the UK takes place at Hampton Court every July. Among the permanent attractions are the over 200-year-old vine and the hedged maze. (Monday 10.15am–6pm, Tuesday to Saturday 9.30am–6pm; in winter until 4.30pm.)

Art History

Roman (1st–4th centuries)

The vast numbers of household artefacts on view in London's museums are proof that *Londinium* was a major centre of Roman civilisation during the occupation. Finds have included writing equipment, fine pottery, cooking and washing utensils and many other items. The Roman historian Tacitus described London in detail. Tertullian (160–230) also mentions the British followers of Christ, so there is good reason to believe that Christianity was well established during Roman times. The excavations of the stone Temple of Mithras in 1954 do, however, indicate that in the 2nd century many Roman soldiers were worshippers of the Asia Minor sun god.

Opposite: St John's Chapel, Tower of London

Roman statue

Anglo-Saxon (4th–10th centuries)

The decline of Roman influence and the migration of the Teutonic Angles, Saxons and Jutes marked a dramatic cultural change. Ornaments and jewellery found in graves, as well as stone markings, demonstrate that even at this period in history there was a demand for the skills of artists and craftsmen. Remains of buildings dating from these times are few and far between. St Stephen's Crypt in the old Palace of Westminster was built in very much the same style as the old Westminster Abbey founded by Edward the Confessor.

Architectural features: crude, flat lintels over windows, doors and arches but with semi-circular or triangular heads. Narrow, sunken windows or double windows with a wide central pillar.

Norman (11th–12th centuries)

William the Conqueror was responsible for the construction of the White Tower fortifications, which were built around 1078. It is easily London's most important monument from the Norman conquest. The Romanesque St John's Chapel in the Tower is certainly the oldest of London's churches. Westminster Hall in the old Palace of Westminster was completed a little later at the end of the 11th century and rebuilt in the 14th century.

Architectural features: thick, round columns or pillars which bear semi-circular arches. Small, rounded windows and small doors, framed with concentric, semi-circular arches and pillars.

The White Tower

Gothic (13th–15th centuries)

Westminster Abbey, which was started in 1245, is the finest example of Early Gothic or Early English ecclesiastical architecture. At around this time, the round Temple Church was also completed. A little later, the church of St Ethel-

Westminster Abbey has
Perpendicular details

dreda (the chapel to the Bishop of Ely's town house) was built in Holborn and is regarded as a masterpiece of Early Decorated style. But the finest example of 14th-century Decorated style is Westminster Hall, which was rebuilt between 1394 and 1398. Its massive oak hammer-beamed roof is the biggest of its kind ever built without supporting pillars – apart, of course, from modern steel and concrete constructions.

The Guildhall and St George's Chapel in Windsor Castle were built in the Late Gothic or Perpendicular style of the 15th century. Henry VII produced the jewel of the age with his Late Perpendicular chapel in Westminster Abbey, not actually completed until 1519, ten years after his death.

Architectural features include the following styles:

Early English: Thin walls with tall, elongated door surrounds and windows often grouped in threes, fives or sevens, the pointed arch and stone pillars surrounded by shafts of Purbeck marble.

Decorated: Pointed spires ornamented with crockets and pinnacles. Complex church vaulting supported by exterior buttresses and slender arcade piers; highly ornate window tracery with each window divided into several lights by mullions.

Perpendicular: Window tracery consisting of vertical members, two- or four- arc arches, lavishly decorated vaults and use of traceried panels.

Literature: Fitzstephen, Thomas Becket's secretary, produced the first description of the City. Geoffrey Chaucer wrote *The Canterbury Tales* and became the 'Father of English Literature'.

Tudor (16th century)

Architectural features: Tudor buildings (1485–1560) strictly speaking followed Gothic style, but at the time of the break with Rome few churches were built. The emphasis was more on castles and country residences. Brick became the usual material, giving speed, good value and flexibility to the building process.

Hampton Court and St James's Palace rank as the finest examples of Tudor architecture – this style was later to become known as Tudor Renaissance or Elizabethan, after Queen Elizabeth I.

Literature: Many new theatres were built in London and the arts, in particular theatre and poetry, were encouraged. John Stow's *Survey of London* was published in 1598 with Stow deserving as much acclaim as a historian as Shakespeare does as a dramatist.

Stuart Renaissance (17th century)

Architectural features: Two distinguished architects left their mark on London during these times: Inigo Jones (1573–1652), who modelled his work on the Italian Andrea Palladio (hence Palladian style), and Sir Christopher Wren (1632–1723), who made a name for himself not only as England's greatest architect, but also as a philosopher and Member of Parliament.

Jones's greatest achievement was the Banqueting Hall in Whitehall Palace. He introduced the Classical style to England and laid the foundations for the later development of English architecture.

After the Great Fire of London, Wren, who was Charles II's chief architect, prepared a plan for rebuilding the whole city, but it was not adopted. Wren, of course, is most famous as the architect of St Paul's Cathedral, which remains such a dominant landmark in London even today. But he was also commissioned to build no less than 51 other churches, each of which left its distinctive mark on the city. His other notable achievements include the Chelsea Hospital, Marlborough House, Kensington Palace, the Monument and the Royal Naval College in Greenwich. His distinctive style is sometimes described as English baroque, but early 17th-century architecture is also known as Jacobean after the reign of James I.

Literature: The celebrated historian Samuel Pepys described contemporary London life between 1600 and 1669 but he is remembered mainly for his diary and his account of the Great Fire and the Great Plague of 1666. Samuel Butler became famous as the Poet of St Paul's and other famous London men of letters include Ben Jonson and John Donne.

Music: Orlando Gibbons, Henry Purcell and later John Blow were the leading London composers of the period.

Windsor's Tudor houses

17th-century Banqueting Hall

Georgian (18th century)

Architectural features: In the years named after George I, George II and George III, the classical features of Wren's architecture were adopted. The best known London architects are William Kent (Horse Guards building), Sir William Chambers (Somerset House), Sir John Soane (Bank of England) and the Adams brothers, Robert and James. Also worthy of mention are George Dance's Mansion House, James Gibbs's baroque Mary-le-Strand and the stone and woodwork of Grinling Gibbons, eg. the choir stalls in St Paul's Cathedral.

Choir stalls, St Paul's
Dr Johnson's house

Literature: Dr Samuel Johnson and his artistic friends left their mark on the literary life of London at this time. Writers such as Dryden, Pope, Swift, Fielding, Smollett and many others were part of his circle. In 1764, together with the painter Sir Joshua Reynolds, he founded the famous Literary Club in Gerrard Street.

Music: The German composers Johann Christian Bach (known as the 'London Bach') and George Frederick Handel both had a major influence on London's musical scene during this period. Handel lived in Brook Street, Mayfair, for nearly 40 years.

The London of John Nash (early 19th century)

Architectural features: During the first half of the 19th century, the face of London was transformed by the architect and town planner John Nash (1752–1835) and one of his pupils Decimus Burton. Nash's most important contributions were his transformation of Buckingham Palace and the landscaping of Regent's Park. He was also responsible for the famous terraces in the vicinity of Regent's Park, including Hanover Terrace, Kent Terrace, Cumberland Terrace and Chester Terrace. All Souls, Marble Arch, Regent Street, Pall Mall and Piccadilly Circus are all part of Nash's legacy.

Nash-designed terrace,
Regent's Park

Painting: Famous painters such as Thomas Gainsborough, John Constable, William Hogarth, Sir Thomas Lawrence and J M W Turner are all associated with the Georgian period.

Victorian (later 19th century)

Architectural features: During Queen Victoria's reign (1837–1901) the capital's architects sought to recreate the splendour of London's finest medieval buildings. The style is often described as 'neo-Gothic' with the Houses of Parliament, the Albert Memorial, the Royal Albert Hall and the Law Courts as just some of the most obvious examples. Sir George Gilbert Scott is remembered as one of the most important Victorian architects.

The influence of the Industrial Revolution led to a juxtaposition of various architectural styles. The huge popu-

lation movements away from the rural areas to the towns resulted in the development of terraced houses which are such a typical feature of English residential areas. On the other hand, the more wealthy sections of the community sought to counter everyday uniformity and the loss of individuality by romanticising the past. Two styles competed with one another: Classicism and neo-Gothic.

Literature: Realism and romanticism competed with one another in the literary world too. In the same century, writers such as Karl Marx and Charles Dickens, who pricked the consciences of the well-off, worked alongside the celebrated Romantics Lord Byron and Lord Tennyson. Dickens's novels gave harrowing accounts of life amongst London's poorest; the most notable is perhaps *Oliver Twist*. Other celebrated works include *Nicholas Nickleby*, *Little Dorrit*, *Bleak House* and *Great Expectations*.

Charles Dickens

Poets and writers such as Robert Browning, Lord Byron, Lord Tennyson, William Thackeray and Charles Lamb worked in London during this period, as did the founder of modern Communism Karl Marx, who died in March 1883 and is buried in Highgate cemetery. The noted writer and philosopher Thomas Carlyle (1795–1881) lived in Chelsea.

Thomas Carlyle

71

20th century

There is no major artistic movement or school which is not represented somewhere in London. Artists from the Commonwealth countries have flocked here either to study or to work, and have joined or founded one of the many flourishing circles which enable artists to develop their talents. London's multitude of museums and galleries enjoy a worldwide reputation.

Important buildings of this century include London University, the Royal Festival Hall, the Barbican, Lloyd's of London building, and the Broadgate complex near Liverpool Street Station, and Canary Wharf Tower in Docklands. In the world of painting and sculpture, London has become a mecca for practitioners and enthusiasts alike, and for musicians it is without doubt one of the world's leading centres with its concert halls, opera houses, ballets and musicals.

Lloyd's of London

Even if all the world's greatest writers and playwrights of this century are not Londoners, the city would probably claim the credit for having recognised their talent and given the public the opportunity to judge them on their merits. Great poets, dramatists and novelists such as T S Eliot, Christopher Fry, W H Auden and Christopher Isherwood thrived in London's literary circles, as did Somerset Maugham, Noel Coward and J B Priestley. The famous Bloomsbury Group included essayist Lytton Strachey and novelist Virginia Woolf.

Museums

The following is a selection of London's more important museums and art galleries together with their opening times. They are listed in alphabetical order with the name of the nearest Underground station. Most museums are closed on Good Friday, Christmas Eve, Christmas Day, Boxing Day and New Year's Day. Other museums are mentioned in the Places section (*pages 14–65*).

The British Museum is king

Tourist information offices (*see page 98*) can provide additional details, but all the latest information on opening times and special exhibitions is included in the weekly London magazines *Time Out* or *What's On*.

British Museum, Great Russell Street, WC1 (nearest Underground stations: *Russell Square, Holborn* or *Goodge Street*). National library and museum of history, archaeology and art (Monday to Saturday 10am–5pm, Sunday 2.30–6pm).

Commonwealth Institute, Kensington High Street, W8 (nearest Underground station: *High Street Kensington*). Permanent exhibitions on the life, history, geography and mineral resources of Commonwealth countries. Audio-visual presentations. Art gallery (Monday to Saturday 10am–5.00pm, Sunday 11am–5pm).

Courtauld Institute Galleries, Somerset House, Strand, WC2 (nearest Underground stations: *Temple, Embankment* or *Charing Cross*). The country's most important collection of Impressionist and late Impressionist paintings (Monday to Saturday 10am–6pm, Sunday 2–6pm).

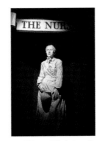

Nurse Nightingale

Florence Nightingale Museum, St Thomas's Hospital, 2 Lambeth Palace Road, SE1 (nearest Underground station: *Westminster*). An account of working conditions for nurses in the last century and how Florence Nightingale changed the profession after her experiences in the Crimean War (Tuesday to Sunday, 10am–4pm).

Freud Museum, 20 Maresfield Gardens, Hampstead, NW3 (nearest Underground station: *Finchley Road*). Home of exiled Sigmund Freud from June 1938 to his death in 1939. Memorabilia includes his psychoanalyst's couch (Wednesday to Sunday noon–5pm).

Hayward Gallery, South Bank, Embankment, SE1 (nearest Underground station: *Waterloo*). Exhibitions organised by the Arts Council, usually of contemporary paintings and sculpture (Monday, Thursday to Sunday 10am–6pm, Tuesday and Wednesday 10am–8pm).

Imperial War Museum, Lambeth Road, SE1 (nearest Underground stations: *Lambeth North* or *Elephant and Castle*). Exhibits from both world wars, collections of aeroplanes, military vehicles, arms, a German one-man U-Boat, documents, etc. A main attraction is the Blitz Experience, a simulation of a London air-raid with realistic lighting and sound effects (daily 10am–6pm).

Exhibits of warfare

Jewish Museum, Woburn House, Upper Woburn Place, WC1 (nearest Underground stations: *Euston* or *Euston Square*). Collection of scrolls and ritual objects (Tuesday to Friday and Sunday, 10am–4pm, in winter Friday and Sunday only 10am–12.45pm).

London Dungeon, 28–34, Tooley Street, SE1 (nearest Underground station: *London Bridge*). A gruesome collection of tableaux with sound effects illustrating medieval torture, witchcraft, the death of Thomas Becket and the start of the Great Fire (daily 10am–5.30pm, in winter 10am–4.30pm).

The London Dungeon

London Toy & Model Museum, 23 Craven Hill, W2 (nearest Underground stations: *Queensway* or *Lancaster Gate*). Toys and model railways from 1850 to the present day, including an old roundabout (Tuesday to Saturday 10am–5.30pm, Sunday 11am–5.30pm).

73

London Transport Museum, Flower Market, WC2 (nearest Underground stations: *Covent Garden* or *Leicester Square*). The development of public transport in London from the horse-drawn carriage to the Underground (daily 10am–6pm).

Madame Tussaud's Wax Museum and Planetarium, Marylebone Road, NW1 (nearest Underground station: *Baker Street*). *See page 55.*

Museum of London, London Wall, EC2 (nearest Underground stations: *Barbican, St Paul's* or *Moorgate*). The history of London from prehistoric times to the present day, including archaeological exhibits, models, costumes, jewellery, royal insignia, toys and discoveries from the excavation of Roman burial grounds (Tuesday to Saturday 10am–6pm, Sunday noon–6pm).

Museum of Mankind, 6 Burlington Gardens, W1 (nearest Underground stations: *Piccadilly Circus* or *Green Park*). Ethnographical division of the British Museum. Temporary exhibitions illustrating ancient and contemporary non-Western cultures (Monday to Saturday 10am–5pm, Sunday 2.30–6pm).

Mankind's many facets

Momi is multimedia

Museum of the Moving Image (MOMI), South Bank Arts Centre, Waterloo, SE1 (nearest Underground stations: *Waterloo* or *Embankment*). Impressive portrayal of the history of film and television, with many interactive displays – you can try reading the news or doing a screen test for a Hollywood movie (daily 10am–6pm).

National Army Museum, Royal Hospital Road, Chelsea, SW3 (nearest Underground station: *Sloane Square*). Pictures, arms, memorabilia and much more on the history of British, Indian and colonial land forces from Tudor times to the present day (daily 10am–5.30pm).

The National's Madonna

National Gallery, Trafalgar Square, WC2 (nearest Underground stations: *Charing Cross* or *Embankment*). Unique collection of Europe's most famous paintings from the 13th to the 20th centuries (Monday to Saturday 10am–6pm, Sunday 2–6pm).

National Portrait Gallery, St Martin's Place, WC2 (nearest Underground stations: *Charing Cross* or *Embankment*). Portraits of famous Britons from Tudor times to the present day (Monday to Friday 10am–5pm, Saturday 10am–6pm, Sunday 2–6pm).

National Postal Museum, King Edward Building, King Edward Street, EC1 (nearest Underground station: *St Paul's*). Collection of British and world stamps (Monday to Friday 9.30am–4.30pm).

Natural History Museum, Cromwell Road, SW7 (nearest Underground station: *South Kensington*). Now merged with the **Geological Museum** and divided into the Life and Earth galleries. History of the earth with human, animal and plant remains, dinosaurs, fossils, minerals and meteorites (Monday to Saturday 10am–5.50pm, Sunday 11am–5.50pm).

Royal Academy of Arts

Queen's Gallery, Buckingham Palace Road, SW1 (nearest Underground station: *Victoria*). Royal collection of paintings, portraits and other art works (Tuesday to Saturday 10am–5pm, Sunday 2–5pm).

Royal Academy of Arts, Burlington House, Piccadilly W1 (nearest Underground stations: *Piccadilly Circus* or *Green Park*). Changing exhibitions, often of contemporary art (Monday to Sunday 10am–6pm).

Science Museum, Exhibition Road, SW7 (nearest Underground station: *South Kensington*). The history of science, medicine and industry with historic cars, trains and aeroplanes. Children's galleries with mechanical and electronic gadgetry. Collection of domestic appliances (Monday to Saturday 10am–6pm, Sunday 11am–6pm).

Serpentine Gallery, Kensington Gardens, W2 (nearest Underground stations: *Lancaster Gate* or *Knightsbridge*). Exhibitions of contemporary art (daily 10am–6pm).

Sir John Soane's Museum, 13 Lincoln's Inn Fields, WC2 (nearest Underground station: *Holborn*). This famous architect's home (18th century) has been faithfully preserved; Soane stipulated that nothing should be moved or altered, so the displays appear cluttered and untidy. The picture gallery includes a number of famous Hogarth paintings (Tuesday to Saturday 10am–5pm, guided tour Saturday 2.30pm).

Tate Gallery, Millbank, SW1 (nearest Underground station: *Pimlico*). British paintings, national collection of 20th-century pictures and sculptures (Monday to Saturday 10am–6pm, Sunday 2–6pm).

75

Theatre Museum, Covent Garden, WC2 (nearest Underground stations: *Covent Garden* or *Leicester Square*). Set within a former market warehouse, it contains the entire theatre collection from the Victoria and Albert Museum and the former British Theatre Museum (Tuesday to Sunday 11am–7pm).

Theatrical artefacts

Tower of London (nearest Underground station: *Tower Hill*). *See page 30.*

Victoria and Albert Museum, South Kensington, SW7 (nearest Underground station: *South Kensington*). A storehouse of the decorative arts with examples from all parts of the world, all periods and in all styles. The museum also houses the National Art Gallery, collections of sculpture from the late Classical period and the works of John Constable. (Monday to Saturday 10am–5.50pm, Sunday 2.30–5.50pm).

The V & A

Wallace Collection, Manchester Square, W1 (nearest Underground station: *Bond Street*). Largest collection of French paintings and *objets d'art* outside France, as well as works by Titian, Rubens and other European masters (Monday to Saturday 10am–5pm, Sunday 2–5pm).

Wellington Museum, Apsley House, Hyde Park Corner, W1 (nearest Underground station: *Hyde Park Corner*). Collection of pictures, porcelain, silver and Duke of Wellington memorabilia (Tuesday to Sunday 11am–5pm).

Music and Theatre

Entertainment for all

London's theatreland centres around Shaftsbury Avenue and Covent Garden where some shows have been running for decades. The official *London Theatre Guide* may be purchased from stations and air terminals and a pocket guide is usually available at information kiosks, good hotels, theatre box offices or theatre ticket agencies. A full listing is also published in the London daily and evening newspapers.

Theatres are closed on Sundays.

West End theatres are popular and tickets are hard to obtain. It is advisable to buy tickets a couple of days in advance either from theatre box offices or one of the many theatre ticket advance booking agencies. If you can't book through the theatre box office (credit card bookings by telephone accepted) try Ticketmaster (tel: 0171-344 4444) and First Call (tel: 0171-240 7200) before going to other agencies who may charge a hefty fee.

On the day of the performance, tickets may be obtained at half price plus a small handling charge at the Half Price Ticket Booth in Leicester Square. It is open from noon to 2pm for matinées and for evening performances from 2.30–6.30pm. If all theatres are sold out, the booth does not open.

Theatre venues

Barbican Theatre (nearest Underground station: *Barbican*) is home to the Royal Shakespeare Company.

The Pit is a smaller studio theatre.

Royal National Theatre, Waterloo Bridge, (nearest Underground station: *Waterloo*). A total of three stages with productions ranging from classical drama to the latest in experimental theatre.

Opera and ballet

London has two large opera houses, with performances throughout the year apart from August. A limited number of tickets are available at both venues from 10am on the morning of the performance.

The Royal Opera House Covent Garden (nearest Underground station: *Covent Garden*) is one of the largest opera houses in the world, attracting the very best singers.

The English National Opera perform in the **London Coliseum** in St Martin's Lane (nearest Underground station: *Charing Cross*) and all operas are sung in English.

Sadler's Wells Theatre (nearest Underground station: *Angel*) is the London theatre for ballet, but both opera houses also give ballet performances. At Sadler's Wells, cut-price tickets for the front few rows are sold from the box office at 10.30am on the day of a performance.

Concerts

The best-known concert halls are the Royal Festival Hall, the Barbican and the Royal Albert Hall, all of which have concerts nearly every night of the year.

The **Royal Festival Hall**, South Bank (nearest Underground station: *Waterloo*) seats 3,000 and is the home of the London Philharmonic Orchestra. It was opened in 1951 to celebrate the Festival of Britain. In the foyer at lunchtimes, there is often a free concert. The Queen Elizabeth Hall and the Purcell Room are both parts of the South Bank arts complex.

The London Symphony Orchestra is based at the **Barbican** (nearest Underground station: *Barbican*).

The famous Promenade concerts ('the Proms'), which are held every year between July and September, take place in the **Royal Albert Hall**, Kensington Gore (nearest Underground station: *South Kensington*).

In the summer months open-air concerts are often held in Holland Park, Marble Hill, Twickenham and by the lake at Kenwood House on Hampstead Heath. Lunchtime concerts are held in the churches of St Martin-in-the-Fields in Trafalgar Square and St John's in Smith Square, SW1.

The weekly magazines *Time Out* and *What's On* give full details of London's concerts.

77

Cinema

For cinema-goers, British premières take place in the large cinemas around Leicester Square. There are several art houses, notably the **National Film Theatre** (nearest Underground station: *Waterloo*) with two screens, plus a cinema in the Museum of the Moving Image.

The Royal Albert Hall

Food and Drink

London is one of the world's great culinary cities. This is partly due to the range of cosmopolitan cuisines available and also due to the fact that the past few years have seen a re-evaluation of Britain's indigenous cuisine. The country's once-scorned reputation for badly cooked, unimaginative, stodgy meals has gradually been overturned by the present generation of innovative chefs.

Be that as it may, the British Isles are too big for there to be a typical British cuisine. England, Scotland and Wales are proud of their own culinary heritage. Cooking traditions in England have developed along two separate lines. An island nation depends on its fishermen and the harvest of the seas has been complemented by the meat and dairy produce of its farmers, but the growth of the empire and the influence of the colonies is reflected in the tastes of the British people. London is not unique in being able to offer a wide choice of international dishes. Nearly every small English town can boast at least one Indian and one Chinese restaurant and many have restaurants serving French- and Italian- style cuisine.

OPEN
SUNDAYS
FOR
TRADITIONAL
ENGLISH
ROAST
LUNCH

79

The English breakfast is world-famous. A guest at a 'bed and breakfast' guest house (*see page 103*) will almost certainly be offered bacon, fried or scrambled eggs with toast, butter and marmalade.

For lunch or dinner, most English restaurants will offer fish, seafood, and almost certainly steak, which is served grilled or lightly fried, so that the inner flesh is still slightly pink. Spicy brown sauce, such as the famous Worcestershire sauce, often accompanies meat.

Fruit 'n' veg for sale

The fertile counties to the south and southwest of London provide the capital with a wide selection of vegetables, which are usually served boiled. If not over-cooked, the vitamins, colour and natural flavour are preserved. The garden of England, Kent, produces fruit with a worldwide reputation, the best-known examples being the Cox apple, the Victoria plum and the Williams pear.

The British dessert ('pudding') is characterised by the pie, a fruit tart with a pastry top to preserve it. Yorkshire pudding, however, is usually served with roast beef and potatoes and is simply a crispy brown ring of baked batter. No traditional British Sunday dinner of roast beef and Yorkshire pudding is complete without gravy, a thickened sauce made from beef stock.

Christmas traditions include plum pudding, otherwise known as Christmas pudding, which should be prepared well in advance of the festive season. Plums, currants, lemon peel, suet and a wide variety of spices are mixed together and boiled for several hours. This is another dish which has nautical origins, being suitable for long jour-

A pleasant snack on the pavement

Eels 'n' edibles

neys. Before serving at Christmas, pour on a little warmed rum or brandy and flambée.

Lamb features on many English menus, some home-produced but much of it imported from New Zealand. The traditional casserole of lamb or mutton called Lancashire hotpot is well worth trying.

The English have always enjoyed fish and no visitor to London should miss an opportunity to try fish and chips, eaten straight from the bag after sprinkling a little salt and vinegar on them. Smoked haddock and kippers (smoked herring) are just two of the many fish dishes which the British have popularised and exported.

The king of English cheeses is Stilton and it is traditionally accompanied by port. It dates from the 16th century and is a blue-veined cheese with a hard crust. Cheddar, with its strong nutty flavour, is a cheese that it is widely copied but nothing can equal a mature English cheddar. Cheshire has a crumbly texture and a milder flavour. A good Cheshire should have matured for at least two years. Wensleydale is another typically English mild cheese with a slightly sweet spiciness.

There are few dishes which can be described as typical Londoners' fare, but fish, shellfish and seafood have always featured prominently on the working family's plate. The following are traditional London dishes, but most will only be found in small neighbourhood cafés.

Eel pie and mash: eel, lemon, parsley and onions served in pastry. Originally it was served with beef stock, but now more commonly with mashed potatoes.

Faggots and peas: stew made from pork, liver, kidneys, onions, sage and rosemary, served with mushy peas.

Pease pudding: a purée of peas made from dried yellow peas, with pieces of boiled ham and fresh herbs, served with carrots and a thick gravy.

Crumpets: a small, spongy yeast cake, which should be served hot and with plenty of butter.

Almost without exception, the British drink tea. Although there are many different blends, each with their own individual serving instructions, it is usually drunk with fresh milk. No other kind of milk is suitable. English beers (which include some remarkable brews such as Theakston's Old Peculier) are undergoing something of a revival – although lager, which is similar to light Continental beers but slightly sweeter, is now consumed in greater quantities than the traditional ales.

Stouts (such as Guinness or Murphy's) are thick, dark beers (*see page 81*). Port, madeira and sherry are popular as aperitifs. Most whiskies come from Scotland and are often drunk with ice and water, although purists drink single-malt whiskies 'neat' (with nothing added). Irish whiskies are also widely available.

Restaurants

There is a restaurant in London to suit every taste and every pocket. Within walking distance of most Underground stations there will be somewhere to try typical English fare, or the more adventurous may choose to take a culinary world tour.

The main concentration of London's restaurants is in the West End with Soho providing the most interesting and widest choice, whilst Covent Garden can offer good pre-theatre suppers. Chinatown, centring around Gerrard Street, is full of Cantonese restaurants. Bayswater also has many good value ethnic restaurants. A good meal out in London can be expensive, reflecting the high cost of living; however, many restaurants provide cheaper menus at lunch-time. Ethnic restaurants provide some of the best value, whereas pubs, wine bars and cafés often serve very good inexpensive snacks. A free leaflet is distributed to most hotels with restaurant recommendations, but an objective guide on where to eat is the *Nicholson London Restaurant Guide* (available from most bookshops).

Hamburger heaven

Before sitting down in a restaurant it is customary to wait for a waiter or waitress to show you to your table, so that you can make any particular requests about seating. Some restaurants invite guests to take an aperitif, perhaps a sherry or a port, while they look at the menu. In other restaurants there is a bar where guests can sit and drink in comfort until the *hors d'oeuvre* is served.

Pubs – an introduction

Pub grub

A visitor to London is never far away from a pub (short for public house). The pub is to London as the street cafés are to Paris, but the Continental beer drinker will be surprised by some of the British customs. While a good head of froth is an important requirement in France, a pint of English beer should have no head and a serious drinker would ask the barman for another pint.

Very few pubs serve tea or coffee but an increasingly wide range of soft drinks is available. There has been a move in recent years to free pubs from the restriction of serving only one brewer's beers and most pubs try to stock as many draught and bottled beers as possible. A pub which is not tied to any one particular brewer is known as a Free House.

There are many more types of beer on sale than in a Continental brasserie or Bierkeller and a drinker who asks for 'a pint of beer' will simply confuse the barman. A *lager* is closest to Continental and American beers, a *stout* is a dark, strong beer, but most seasoned British drinkers drink *bitter*, a light brown beer which should taste fresh, hoppy, with no fizzy gas and is never chilled but served at room temperature. A pint is just over half a litre (0.568l) and

Pulling the pints

many people order a half, instead of a full pint. It is not advisable to find a seat and wait for the waiter. In every pub in Great Britain, the customer orders his or her drink at the bar and pays for it immediately. As a general rule, it is not necessary to tip but some regular drinkers offer to buy the barman or barmaid a drink.

Most pubs in London consist of more than one room and almost certainly have more than one entrance. One will lead to the public bar which will be furnished simply and is usually a man's world, while couples or unaccompanied women are more likely to use the lounge, which is usually more comfortably furnished and carpeted.

Pubs usually offer food. Look for a sign outside which says 'pub grub'; this generally means food bought over the bar rather than an elaborate restaurant-style meal and the microwave oven usually plays a significant role. In London the meals on offer at lunchtimes offer the best value and are often typical British dishes. Bangers and mash (fried sausages and mashed potato), bubble and squeak (mixture of cabbage, onions and potato with cold meat), Scotch eggs (hard-boiled egg rolled in sausage meat and breadcrumbs), ploughman's lunch (Cheddar cheese, bread and mixed pickles), steak and kidney pie, and sausage roll are all traditional pub fare, although many pubs are now beginning to offer a wider and more adventurous selection of food.

82

Children under the age of 14 are not allowed in pubs and no alcoholic drinks may be served to anyone under the age of 18.

The pub is to London as the street cafés are to Paris

Normal opening times are Monday to Saturday 11am–11pm, Sunday 11am–3pm and 7–10.30pm.

Restaurant selection
Traditional British restaurants

Simpsons-in-the-Strand, 100 Strand WC2, tel: 0171-836 9112. Renowned for serving the best roast beef in London. Staunchly traditional. Expensive.

The Quality Chop House, 94 Farringdon Road EC1, tel: 0171-837 5093. A 19th-century City clerks' dining room with its original fixed wooden seating intact. Expensive.

Modern British

Alastair Little, 49 Frith Street W1, tel: 0171-734 5183. Imaginative and eclectic food within tasteful surroundings. Expensive.

Baboon, Jason Court, 76 Wigmore Street W1, tel: 0171-224 2992. Serves superb, well thought-out modern British food based around traditional recipes. Expensive.

Sunday Lunch

Wilson's, 236 Blythe Road W14, tel: 0171-603 7267. One of the best Sunday lunches in town, with consistently high quality in this dignified restaurant. Quite expensive.

The English House, 3 Milner Street SW3. tel: 0171-584 3002. Quaint English dining room within a pretty Chelsea town house. Quite expensive.

American Theme

Dashing for lunch

Hard Rock Café, 150 Old Park Lane W1, tel: 0171-629 0382. A shrine to rock music, serving some of the best burgers in town. Great fun. Quite expensive.

Rock Island Diner, London Pavilion, Piccadilly Circus W1, tel: 0171-287 5500. Fun and loud 1950s-style diner kitted out with kitsch décor. Quite expensive.

Places to be Seen

The Ivy, 1 West Street WC2, tel: 0171-836 4751. High quality décor, and well thought out food. Expensive.

Kensington Place, 201 Kensington Church Street W8, tel: 0171-727 3184. Trendy and informal, this New York-style restaurant is always busy. Expensive.

Langhan's Brasserie, Stratton Street W1, tel: 0171-491 8822. Langhan's large reputation for attracting celebrities often overshadows the food. Michael Caine is part owner of this fashionable brasserie. Expensive.

Some traditional pubs

The Anchor, 1 Bankside SE1 (riverside).
The Black Friar, 174 Queen Victoria Street EC4.
The Dickens Inn, St Katharine's Way E1 (riverside).
Ye Olde Cheshire Cheese, 145 Fleet Street EC4.
The Spaniard's Inn, Hampstead Lane NW3.
The Dove, 19 Upper Mall W6 (riverside).

Shopping and Markets

Shopping hours

As a rule, London shops are open from 9am to 5.30pm. Some shops in Knightsbridge, Sloane Square and King's Road stay open until 7pm on Wednesday. In Regent Street and Oxford Street, many shops stay open until 7pm on Thursday. Many supermarkets stay open until 8pm and in most parts of London there are small grocers' shops which stay open until 10pm. Shops in Covent Garden are also open until 8pm.

Shops are open all day on Saturday. The Berwick Street fruit and vegetable market in Soho is open on weekdays from 8am to 5pm.

Window dressing

Shopping streets

The main shopping streets are situated inside the Underground Circle line. *See Underground map page 96.*

Oxford Street (nearest Underground stations: *Marble Arch, Bond Street, Oxford Circus* or *Tottenham Court Road*). London's busiest and most popular shopping street is on the western side of Marble Arch and extends as far as Tottenham Court Road. As well as dozens of menswear and women's fashion shops, Oxford Street also has a number of major department stores including Marks & Spencer and London's second biggest department store, Selfridges. A tourist information office is located in the basement of Selfridges.

Regent Street crosses Oxford Street at Oxford Circus. High-class shops sell quality fashions, textiles, porcelain and jewellery. Liberty's is renowned for its fabrics.

Bond Street elegance

Bond Street, New Bond Street and Old Bond Street (nearest Underground stations: *Bond Street* or *Green Park*). Bond Street is at the up-market end of London's shopping centres with expensive, high-quality fashion shops, exclusive beauty salons, antiques shops, etc.

Piccadilly (nearest Underground station: *Knightsbridge*). Look out for royal suppliers Fortnum and Mason and the Burlington Arcade, a covered shopping mall with a range of exclusive shops.

The western end of Piccadilly becomes **Knightsbridge** (nearest Underground station: *Knightsbridge*). Another elegant shopping centre dominated by Harrods, the biggest and most famous department store in Europe. Brompton Road and Sloane Street which branch off to the south are also popular shopping streets.

Kensington High Street (nearest Underground station: *High Street Kensington*) has for many years competed with Carnaby Street as the centre for the latest designs. Dozens of fashionable boutiques for men and women.

Kensington Church Street (nearest Underground station: *High Street Kensington*) is the mecca of the antiques world, but there are also many clothes shops catering for the fashion-conscious.

King's Road (nearest Underground station: *Sloane Square*) is Chelsea's main street. Formerly at the heart of London's 'Swinging Sixties' and later the territory of London's punk rockers, it is now the most fashionable place in the capital to buy and show off designer clothes. Clothing stores predominate, but there are plenty of antiques arcades and art galleries – although it is not the best place to look for a bargain. Saturday afternoon is the time to take a stroll down the King's Road and look out for famous faces.

Charing Cross Road (nearest Underground station: *Tottenham Court Road*) links the end of Oxford Street with Trafalgar Square and is famous for its bookstores. Antiquarian bookshops and major book retailers combine to create an ideal place for browsing.

Information centres

The Design Council, 28 Haymarket, SW1 (nearest Underground station: *Piccadilly Circus*) regularly holds exhibitions of British design. In addition, the centre has one of the biggest bookshops in Europe specialising in design (Monday to Saturday 10am-6pm, Sunday 1–6pm). **Contemporary Applied Arts**, 43 Earlham Street, WC2 (nearest Underground station: *Covent Garden* or *Leicester Square*) is also an exhibition and sales centre for British crafts (admission free).

Department stores

Fortnum and Mason, 181 Piccadilly, W1 (nearest Underground stations: *Green Park* or *Piccadilly Circus*).

Harrods, Knightsbridge, SW1 (nearest Underground station: *Knightsbridge*).

Liberty's, 210–220 Regent Street, W1 (nearest Underground station: *Oxford Circus*).

Marks & Spencer, 458 Oxford Street, W1 (nearest Underground station: *Marble Arch*).

Marks & Spencer, 103–105 Kensington High Street, W8 (nearest Underground station: *High Street, Kensington*).

Selfridges, 400 Oxford Street, W1 (nearest Underground station: *Marble Arch*).

Street markets

There are more than 100 markets in London, carrying on a tradition which goes back to the city's earliest days. Many of them are open daily, but there are some which are only open on certain days of the week or at the weekend. A leaflet available from the London Tourist Board & Con-

A neat hat-trick

Liberty's of London

Portobello Road stall

Petticoat Lane

vention Bureau, entitled *Street Markets*, gives details of London's many different markets.

One of the daily markets is in **Berwick Street**, although it overflows into some of the neighbouring streets (closed Thursday afternoon and Sunday). Another market which is open every day except Monday is in **East Street Lane** (nearest Underground station: *Elephant & Castle*). Stalls are generally open 8.30am–5.30pm and on Sunday mornings until 1pm.

Petticoat Lane Market, Middlesex Street, E1. The district of Houndsditch, where Middlesex Street lies, is the centre for Jewish traders. As Jews are traditionally not allowed to work on the Sabbath (Saturday), this market opens on Sunday morning from 9am to 2pm (nearest Underground stations: *Liverpool Street, Aldgate* or *Aldgate East*). Petticoat Lane has become such a popular market that on many Sundays it is almost impossible to move in the desired direction. It is easier to go with the crowd, but this brings the danger of pickpockets so be careful if carrying valuables. The market attracts photographers as many of the market traders and shoppers are local Cockney characters. The stalls sell everything from fruit, vegetables and household items to clothes and jewellery. Despite attracting many tourists, Petticoat Lane is a genuine market where local people shop.

Portobello Road, W11 (nearest Underground stations: *Ladbroke Grove* or *Notting Hill Gate*) is another of London's famous street markets (Monday to Saturday 9am–5pm, Thursday 9am–1pm). On weekdays the market sells fruit, vegetables and flowers, but on Saturday its character changes and from 8am, sometimes even 7am, until 5 or 6pm, everything imaginable is on sale, even rare antiques, although they are often at inflated prices. The quick-witted traders and their cosmopolitan customers – millions of them, it often seems on a Saturday – give this market a special allure.

The market at **Camden Lock**, NW1 (nearest Underground station: *Camden Town*) is open on Saturday and Sunday from 8.30am to 5.30 or 6pm. Stalls at the nearby market on Camden High Street sell mainly goods imported from Third World countries, but also a wealth of good-quality handmade items. In places the market resembles a flea market, with second-hand goods and bric-a-brac on sale. The best day for clothes is Sunday. Behind the market are a number of workshops and studios where visitors can watch the craftsmen at work. The setting for this market on the bank of Regent's Canal helps to create a very pleasant atmosphere.

The **Jubilee Market** at Covent Garden has become a major attraction in recent years. From 9am to about 4.30pm the market stalls offer different goods depending on the day of the week. Monday is an antiques fair, Tuesday and Friday second-hand goods are on sale and on Sunday there is a craft fair.

Other London antiques markets include:

87

Bermondsey Antiques Market (often still known as the New Caledonian Market), situated on the corner of Long Lane and Bermondsey Street, SE1 (nearest Underground station: *London Bridge*). Friday is the best day to go on an antiques treasure hunt starting at 6am and continuing until about 2pm. The early opening time is significant as it indicates that many of the stalls are run by wholesalers who sell their goods early in the day to other traders who then resell them to the visiting tourists. The enormous selection of second-hand goods ranges from junk to jewellery.

Bermondsey Antiques Market

Camden Passage Market (nearest Underground station: *Angel*) is a mixture of shops and stalls and has acquired a reputation for good-value antiques (Wednesday and Saturday 8am–5pm).

Chelsea Antiques Market in the King's Road, SW3 (nearest Underground station: *Sloane Square*) often consists of more than 100 stalls and is open from Monday to Saturday 10am–6pm. There is a good chance of picking up a bargain.

Aladdin's Cave in the cellar of the London Silver Vaults in Chancery Lane, WC2 (nearest Underground station: *Chancery Lane*) probably houses the biggest collection of silver in the world. The items on sale range from genuine antique silver to modern jewellery and cutlery. The 50 or so dealers operate from rooms which resemble strongrooms, from Monday to Friday 9am–5.30pm and Saturday 9am–12.30pm.

A night on the town

Nightlife

London offers a tremendous range of evening entertainment, with music-lovers particularly well catered for. Soho is the area for strip clubs, with Raymond's Revue Bar in Brewer Street probably the best-known, but there are many other clubs and pubs in that part of the city which are popular haunts for contemporary music fans.

Again, *Time Out* and *What's On* are the best sources of information on jazz, pop and folk music evenings.

Ronnie Scott's, 47 Frith Street, W1 (nearest Underground stations: *Leicester Square, Tottenham Court Road* or *Piccadilly Circus*) is the best-known jazz club.

The 100 Club at 100 Oxford Street (nearest Underground station: *Oxford Circus*) is a popular venue for jazz, swing and rockabilly. Sunday to Wednesday open until midnight, Thursday and Saturday until 1am, Friday until 3am.

Many pubs have regular jazz nights. Try **The Bull's Head** (373 Lonsdale Road, SW13), **The Bull and Gate** (389 Kentish Town Rd, NW5) or **The Torrington** (4 Lodge Lane, N12).

Some pubs specialise in folk music nights. **The Weavers Arms** (98 Newington Green Rd, NW1), **Sir George Robey** (240 Seven Sisters Road, N4) and **Half Moon** (93 Lower Richmond Road, SW15) are all popular haunts. **Bunjie's** (27 Litchfield Street, WC2) is a folk club near Leicester Square.

The best way to find out about the many pop, rock and soul concerts is to buy one of the London listings magazines. Well known venues include the **Apollo Hammersmith** (Queen Caroline Street, W6), the **Academy Brixton** (211 Stockwell Road, SW9) and the **Rock Garden** (The Piazza, Covent Garden, WC2).

Of course, there are discotheques in all parts of London. The **Hippodrome** near Leicester Square is one of the biggest in the world and it is very popular with young visitors to the city. For somewhere a little more exclusive and expensive, try **Stringfellows** (16 Upper St Martin's Lane, WC2). **Le Palais** in Hammersmith (Hammersmith Broadway, W6) has been refurbished and re-opened as a discotheque.

There are also a number of night spots which combine dining and dancing, including **Barbarella** (428 Fulham Road, SW6), the exclusive **Concordia Notte** (29–31 Craven Road, W2) and the **Elephant on the River** (129 Grosvenor Road, SW1). Dance music bands play during dinner at most of the luxury hotels. Tea dances in the Thirties style are held most Sunday afternoons at the Palm Court in the Waldorf Hotel, Aldwych. A telephone call for further details is advisable.

Recreation

Olde England

In recent years a taste has developed for Elizabethan banqueting halls, which offer guests the opportunity to indulge themselves in Tudor style. Staff dress up in period costume and diners are entertained by minstrels, dancers and troubadours while they eat.

Hatfield House on the northern outskirts of London is one such place for a step back in time. In the City, try **The Beefeater by the Tower** (St Katharine's Dock, E1).

Olde Worlde entertainment

Something of the atmosphere of the 18th- and 19th-century music hall is conveyed at the **Cockney Cabaret and Music Hall** (161 Tottenham Court Road, W1) or **Tiddy Dols Eating House** (2 Hertford Street, W1).

Canal trips

Very few tourists are aware of the pleasure cruises along the Regent's Canal.

Jason's Trip lasts 90 minutes and covers the prettiest section of the canal. Boats leave from opposite 60 Bloomfield Road (nearest Underground station: *Warwick Avenue*). The company also organises evening cruises for private parties, tel: 0171-286 3428.

Cruising the canals

Jenny Wren trips leave from Camden Lock on the Regent's Canal, pass through London Zoo in Regent's Park and round the island at Little Venice (90 minutes).

This company organises Sunday lunch and evening cruises. Book in advance, tel: 0171-485 4433. Boats leave from Camden Lock, 250 Camden High Street, NW1 (nearest Underground station: *Camden Town*).

The vessels of the London Waterbus Company not only ply the Regent's Canal; the day-trip to the River Lea is a journey through the industrial and architectural history of London's canals, tel: 0171-482 2550.

Families with young children

Childminders (tel: 0171-935 9763/935 2049) or Universal Aunts (tel: 0171-738 8937) can arrange babysitters and nannies for visitors.

London Tourist Board & Convention Bureau (*see page 98*) has helpful leaflet, *London for Children*.

One of the prettiest lakes in London is in St James's Park near Buckingham Palace and Green Park has some magnificent old trees. The Serpentine is a lake in Hyde Park while to the south, Rotten Row, a riding promenade, links Hyde Park to Kensington Gardens with its attractive Round Pond and the statue of Peter Pan. London Zoo in Regent's Park offers pony rides. Further out of town are the beautiful gardens at Kew, Richmond Park, Hampton Court, Bushey and Greenwich.

Peter Pan and friend

Where children are welcome:

London Zoo (Regent's Park, NW1). Major zoo, with special facilities for children.

Little Angel Marionette Theatre (14 Dagmar Passage, N1). London's best-known puppet theatre with performances on weekdays at 3pm during school holidays, every weekend Saturday 11am and 3pm, Sunday 3pm. Booking is advisable, tel: 0171-226 1787).

Pollock's Toy Museum

Pollock's Toy Museum (1 Scala Street, W1). Toy museum with dolls, puppet theatre and teddy bears (Monday to Saturday 10am–5pm).

Bethnal Green Museum of Childhood (Cambridge Heath Road, E2). Old dolls, dolls' houses, rocking horses, teddy bears, etc. (Monday to Saturday 10am–5.50pm, Sunday 2.30–5.50pm).

London Toy and Model Museum (23 Craven Hill, W2). *See page 73.*

Science Museum (Exhibition Road, SW7). Old railway locomotives, boats and machines with special children's section. *See pages 51 and 74.*

Polka Children's Theatre (240 The Broadway, SW19). Children's theatre, exhibitions of dolls and toys, adventure room (Tuesday to Friday 10am–4.30pm, Saturday 11.30am–6.30pm). Booking is advisable, tel: 0181-543 4888.

Guinness World of Records (Trocadero, Piccadilly, W1). Records detailed in the *Guinness Book of Records* come to life on video (daily 10am–10pm).

Madame Tussaud's Waxwork Museum and Planetarium (Marylebone Rd, NW1). *See page 73.*

Off with their heads! A favourite with children and ideal for a day trip is

Monsters' Retreat at Crystal Palace, which is situated 8 miles (11km) to the south. It is a sculpture park containing models of dinosaurs and other extinct and living reptiles. There is also a children's zoo. 15 miles (23km) to the southwest of London is the **Chessington World of Adventure**, (Leatherhead Rd, Chessington), 65 acres (26 ha) of amusement park and zoo, tel: 037-272 7227.

Recreation

London is richly endowed with all kinds of recreational facilities. For outdoor enthusiasts, it is possible to hire rowing boats in Hyde Park and Regent's Park; Richmond Park and Wimbledon Common are well-suited for horse-ridng. Many suburbs have golf courses. The city also has many facilities for sports such as squash and tennis.

Participatory sport

Most parks have tennis courts, many provide bowling greens and a few have putting greens. Hyde Park and Regent's Park have rowing boats for hire. Richmond Park and Wimbledon Common are well-suited for horse-riding. These swimming pools are recommended: the Oasis Sports Centre, 32 Endell Street, High Holborn, WC2; Porchester Centre, Queensway, WC2; Seymour Leisure Centre, Seymour Place, W1; Swiss Cottage Sports Centre, Winchester Road, NW3; Chelsea Sports Centre, Chelsea Manor Street, SW3.

There are two ice-skating rinks: the Queen's Ice Skating Club, Queensway, W2 and the Alexandra Palace Ice Rink, Wood Green, N22. At the latter, there are facilities for ice-hockey, curling and ice discos.

Squash courts that are open to the public include Medina Rajneesh Body Centre, 81 Belsize Park Gardens, NW3; Dolphin Square, Chichester Street, SW1 and the Finsbury Leisure Centre, Norman Street, EC1.

Guest membership entitles visitors to play indoor tennis at the Vanderbilt Racquet Club, 31 Sterne Street, W12, tel: 0181-743 9822.

There are many suburban golf courses. The following are south of the Thames: Croydon, Dulwich, Sydenham Hill, Wimbledon, Malden, Mitcham, Purley, Richmond Park, Roehampton, Epsom, Bromley, Coulsdon and Osterley. North of the Thames are Brent Valley, Hatfield, Bush Hill Park, Enfield, Ealing, Finchley, Greenford, Barnet, Hampstead, Hendon, Highgate, Kingston-on-Thames, Mill Hill, Muswell Hill, Potters Bar, Stanmore, Strawberry Hill, Twickenham, Wanstead and Sudbury.

Many courses have membership waiting lists, so it is often impossible to play at the weekend. Some clubs ask visitors for a written reference from their usual club. It is advisable in nearly all cases to phone for information.

Running in Richmond

Getting There

By air

Most international airlines operate daily scheduled flights to London, but travel agents and airline companies will advise about the fares and conditions. Travel agents will advise on the availability of charter flights.

Heathrow Airport

The airport is situated on the A4, 15 miles (22km) west of Hyde Park Corner. There are good Underground and bus links into central London. Tourist information and accommodation service available.

Underground: There are two Underground stations at Heathrow. Heathrow Central serves Terminals 1, 2 and 3, Heathrow West serves Terminal 4. Both stations are on the Piccadilly line and the journey to the city centre takes about 40 minutes. The cheapest way to the centre.

Airbus: The A1 and A2 airbuses run every 20 or 30 minutes. The A1 runs from Heathrow to Victoria Station via Cromwell Road and Hyde Park Corner. The A2 runs between Heathrow and Euston Station via Holland Park Avenue, Notting Hill Gate, Bayswater Road, Marble Arch, Bloomsbury and Russell Square.

Gatwick Airport

The airport lies 25 miles (40km) south of London and Gatwick Express trains run from Victoria Station to the airport every 15 minutes or every hour at night. The journey takes 30 minutes. There is also a good bus service, the Green Line 777 Flight Line Service. Tourist information service available.

City Airport

In the Docklands area on the opposite bank of the Thames to Greenwich, a new city centre airport was opened in November 1987 with daily flights to the Continent. There is an Underground connection from Silvertown station and shuttle buses run between Canary Wharf (on the Docklands Light Railway) and the City Airport. As there is a yet relatively little traffic through the airport, check-in times are shorter than at Heathrow or Gatwick.

On the right track

By train

For visitors coming from the Continent, ferries from Belgium, Holland or France usually connect with trains to Victoria or Liverpool Street. Travellers under the age of 26 may buy an InterRail pass – valid for one month's travel on all European railways.

'Eurostar' services operate through the Channel Tunnel from Paris and Brussels, arriving at Waterloo.

By Europabus
Harris Coaches, Manor Road, West Thurrock (tel: 0708-86 4911) are British agents for a Continental coach company which runs services to and from London. Any national travel bureau will provide information on other cross-Channel coaches.

By car
Car ferries to the UK leave from most European countries which have North Sea or English Channel ports. The busiest English port is Dover where ferries from Ostend and Calais arrive after a relatively short crossing. The hovercraft service (Dover–Calais, Dover–Boulogne) and the new Seacat catamaran (Dover–Calais, Folkestone–Boulogne) offer the quickest crossings. 'Le Shuttle' services through the Channel Tunnel offer a speedy alternative. Dover is 71 miles (115km) from London.

Motorists who do not possess a British driving licence should carry the relevant document issued by their government. A 'green card' which extends their insurance to cover other countries is not obligatory, but nevertheless recommended. In Britain, cars drive on the left-hand side of the road and drivers should normally give way to traffic coming from the right.

Drivers and front-seat passengers must wear seat belts. Passengers in the rear of a car must wear seat belts if they are fitted to the car. Motorcyclists must wear crash helmets.

Mapping it out

Getting Around

Driving in London
If you're staying only a short while in the Greater London area, and are unfamiliar with the geography of the capital, don't hire a car. Central London is now more than ever a nightmare to drive in, with its web of one-way streets, bad signposting, and impatient drivers who will cut you up at the first hesitation (taxi drivers in particular seem to regard hesitation as virtually a capital offence).

Meter maid

Parking is a major problem in congested central London. Meters are slightly cheaper than NCP car parks, but only allow parking for a maximum of two or four hours. Most meter parking is free after 6.30pm, after 1.30pm in most areas on Saturday afternoons and all day Sunday. However, always check the details given on the meter.

Don't leave your car on a double yellow line. If you escape a ticket, it is probably because you have been clamped instead. Clamping, whereby your car is rendered immobile until you pay to have it released, is now an epidemic in London. If your car disappears, consult a policeman as it will most likely have been towed away to a car pound. Retrieving it is expensive.

When driving in England you should drive on the left-hand side of the road and observe the speed limits: 30mph (50kph) in urban areas (unless otherwise indicated). 60mph (100kph) on normal roads away from built-up areas and 70mph (112kph) on motorways and dual carriageways (divided highways).

It is strictly illegal to drink and drive and penalties are severe. The law also states that drivers and passengers (front-seat and back-seat) must wear seat belts. Failure to do so can result in a fine. For further information on driving in Britain consult a copy of the *Highway Code*, a booklet which is widely available in bookshops.

All tourist information offices issue free maps showing Underground, bus and train routes, plus other information relating to travel in the London area.

London Underground

The Underground is by far the quickest way to get around. Trains run between 5.30am (Sunday 7.30am) to just before midnight. Underground stations can be identified by a red circle with a thick blue horizontal line which bears the word 'Underground'. Prices vary according to distance and tickets may be purchased from a booking office or a ticket machine. The ticket should be retained until the end of the journey and handed over to the ticket collector or inserted in a machine at the exit barrier.

Buses

To stop a bus, hold your arm out horizontally as the bus approaches. This is particularly important if the bus stop is marked 'Request'.

95

Underground culture

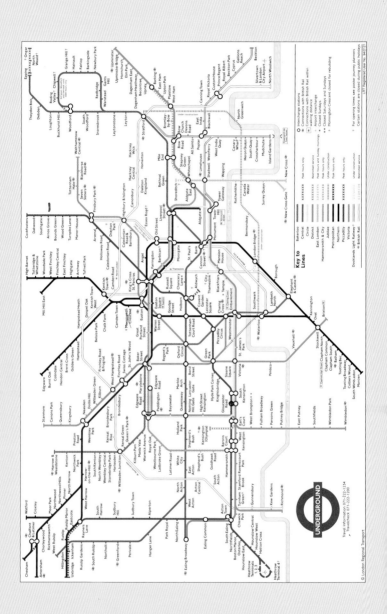

Key to Lines

Bakerloo	
Central	
Circle	
District	
East London	
Hammersmith & City	
Jubilee	
Metropolitan	
Northern	
Piccadilly	
Victoria	
Docklands Light Railway†	
British Rail	

⊖ Interchange stations
⊖ Connections with British Rail

⊖ Connections with British Rail within walking distance

⊖ Airport interchange
* Closed Sundays
** Closed Saturdays and Sundays
✠ Closed Sundays
† Peak hours only

✕✕✕✕✕✕ Peak hours only
✕✕✕✕✕✕ Restricted service
✕✕✕✕✕✕ Peak and Sunday mornings
✕✕✕✕✕✕ Closed Sundays
••••••••• Under construction
✕✕✕✕✕✕ Peak hours only

✕ For opening times see poster journey planners
Certain stations are closed during public holidays

† For opening times see poster journey planners
Certain stations are closed for rebuilding

LRT Registered User No. 94/2121

UNDERGROUND

Travel Information 071-222-1234
Travelcheck 071-222-1200

© London Regional Transport

There are 129 red bus routes, numbered up to 300. They run between 6.30am and 11pm. The quicker Red Arrow buses are usually single-deckers, numbered from 500. They call only at stops serving main shopping centres and stations. An all-night service runs between the centre and the outer suburbs, but buses are less frequent.

Apart from the buses which serve the urban areas, there are also the green Country Buses, numbered from 300 to 499 and from 800. These buses rarely stop within the confines of the city as they link London with places outside the main conurbation. Green Line Coaches, numbered from 701 to 799, serve the outlying areas.

Tourist passes

Visitors who are likely to be on the move for most of their stay are advised to buy a London Visitor Travelcard, which offers more or less unlimited use of the red buses (inside a restricted zone) and the Underground. It is valid for use between the city centre and Heathrow but not on the Airbus. They may be purchased for 1, 3, 4 or 7 days. The card comes with discount vouchers for certain tourist attractions.

There are two other options for visitors: the Travelcard (photo required), available for 7-day or 30-day periods, allows for unlimited travel on buses and the Underground inside a specific zone shown on the ticket. The Off-Peak Travelcard is valid for one day from 9.30am onwards and is the most economical way to get around.

Taxis

A taxi may be hailed if the yellow 'For Hire' sign is lit. The black cabs (other colours are possible) are licensed cabs and are recommended, but fares can be high. The driver is obliged to take you where you want to go provided the journey is less than 6 miles (9km). Supplements are charged for excess luggage and after midnight, on Bank Holidays and weekends with a surcharge for each person carried. A tip of at least 10 percent is usual.

An enduring symbol

Sightseeing tours

Evan Evans Tours Ltd, Richmond (tel: 0181-332 2222), London Cityrama, Silverthorne Rd (tel: 0171-720 6663), Frames Rickards, 11 Herbrand Street (tel: 0171-837 3111), Original London Sightseeing Transport Tours, Wandsworth (tel: 0171-828 7395) offer tours.

A sky-high view

Get to know London on foot with Original London Walks, PO Box 1708, NW6 1PQ (tel: 0171-624 3978) or Citisights of London, 213 Brooke Road (tel: 0181-806 4325) which specialises in London's history. The Londoner Pub Walks, 3 Springfield Ave (tel: 0181-883 2656), organises walking tours to ancient hostelries.

Facts for the Visitor

Currency

Great Britain has a decimal currency. There are 100 pence (p) in one pound sterling (£). There are the following banknotes: £5, £10, £20, £50, and the following coins: 1p, 2p, 5p, 10p, 20p, 50p and £1. The current rate of the pound to other currencies is shown in all banks.

There is no limit on the amount of money, whether sterling or foreign currencies, which may be exported or imported. All banks will change Eurocheques and traveller's cheques. Credit cards such as American Express, Mastercard and Visa are popular and readily accepted in most shops, department stores, hotels and restaurants.

Most banks are open Monday to Friday 9.30am–4.30pm; some are also open on Saturday mornings.

Embassies and High Commissions

Australian High Commission, Australia House, The Strand, WC2; tel: 0171-379 4334.

Canadian High Commission, 38 Grosvenor Street, W1; tel: 0171-629 9492.

Irish Embassy, 17 Grosvenor Square, SW1; tel: 0171-235 2171.

US Embassy

US Embassy, 24 Grosvenor Square, W1; tel: 0171-499 9000.

Entrance regulations

Passport holders from most European countries, the Americas, South Africa, Japan, and most Commonwealth countries do not generally require a visa to enter the UK for a short stay. If in doubt check with the British Embassy in your home country.

Tourist Information Offices

The British Tourist Authority (BTA) has an office or an agency in most countries and brochures and information may be obtained on request.

In London, the British Travel Centre is situated at 12 Regent Street, south of Piccadilly Circus. The British Tourist Authority, British Rail, American Express and Roomcentre all operate from this central office and are able to provide a comprehensive service which includes hotel booking, changing money, information, brochures, maps and souvenirs (Monday to Friday 9am–6.30pm, Saturday and Sunday 10am–4pm).

The headquarters of the London Tourist Board and Convention Bureau (LTB) is at 26 Grosvenor Gardens, Victoria, London SW1W 0DU. Enquiries to this address can only be made in writing. The London Tourist Board's Phone Guide to London offers a complete 24-hour recorded information service to visitors, divided into a total 35 categories. Dial 0839 123 followed by the service selection number, for example: changing of the guards (411); what's on this week (400); what to do on Sunday (407); where to take children (424); London's theatre (423); popular attraction (480); advice on where to stay (435); current exhibitions (403). Visitors can obtain a complete list of the categories and service selection numbers by calling 071-971 0026.

The LTB maintains an information centre and accommodation service on Victoria Station forecourt (Monday to Saturday 8am–7pm, Sunday 8am–4pm), in Selfridges department store basement, Oxford Street (store opening times), at Liverpool Street Station (Monday 8.15am–7pm, Tuesday to Saturday 8.15am–6pm, Sunday 8.30am–4.45pm) and at Heathrow Airport with accommodation service, Terminals 1, 2, 3 Underground station concourse (daily 8am–6pm).

Information for the handicapped: tel: 0171-388 2227 (Monday to Friday 10am–5pm).

Lost property in London
The London Transport Lost Property Office, 200 Baker Street, NW1 (Monday to Friday 9.30am–2pm) will return articles left on London buses or the Underground, but enquiries must be made in person or in writing.

The Metropolitan Police Lost Property Office, 15 Penton Street, N1 looks after articles lost on London taxis, but will only accept enquiries in writing.

For property left on Green Line or London Country Buses, tel: 0181-668 7261 (Monday to Friday 8am–8.30pm, Saturday and Sunday 9am–5pm).

British Railways: enquire at relevant station.

In all other cases, contact any police station or the place where the article was lost, e.g. airport.

Bobbies on the beat

Holidays
The following days are Bank Holidays in England and Wales: 1 January (New Year's Day), Good Friday, Easter Monday, the first Monday in May (May Day), the last Monday in May (Spring Bank Holiday), the last Monday in August, Christmas Day and Boxing Day. If a Bank Holiday falls on a Saturday or a Sunday, then the following Monday becomes the Bank Holiday.

Car hire
Avis, Budget, Godfrey Davis, and Hertz are the major car hire firms and their phone numbers can be found in any phone book. In the capital, problems with parking can cause great difficulties and it is seldom worthwhile hiring a car for London alone.

To rent a car in Britain you must be over 21 years old and must have held a valid, full driving licence for more than a year. The cost of hiring a car will usually include insurance and unlimited free mileage. It does not, however, include insurance cover for accidental damage to interior trim, wheels and tyres or insurance for other drivers without prior approval. Weekly hire rates start at around £170. It can be worth shopping around as some companies offer special weekend and holiday rates.

Car rental companies: The following selection are all members of the London Tourist Board:

Europcar Interrent, tel: 0171-834 8484 (SW1)

Alamo Car Rentals, tel: 0171-408 1255 (SW1)

Eurodollar, tel: 0171-730 8773 (SW1)

Hertz Rentacar, tel: 0171-679 1799

Avis, tel: 0171-848 8733.

For further information, contact the British Travel Centre (*see page 98*) which issues a leaflet, *Vehicle Hire*.

Medical assistance

Help is at hand

If you fall ill and are an EU national, you are entitled to free medical treatment for illnesses arising while in the UK. Many other countries also have reciprocal arrangements for free treatment. However, most visitors will be liable for medical and dental treatment and should ensure they have adequate health insurance before leaving home.

In the case of a serious accident or emergency, dial 999. In the case of minor accidents, your hotel will know the location of the nearest hospital with a casualty department. If you sprain your wrist in the street, hail a cab. Amazingly, cab drivers seem to know just about everything.

Chemists: Boots is a large chain of pharmacies with numerous branches throughout London that will make up prescriptions. The branch at 75 Queensway, W2 is open until 10pm daily while Bliss Chemist at Marble Arch is open until midnight daily.

Opening times

Shop and office hours in London are usually Monday to Friday 9 or 9.30am–5.30pm. Shops in the centre of town rarely close for lunch and may stay open later, particularly around Covent Garden and Piccadilly Circus. Increasing numbers of shops are open on Sunday, particularly supermarkets and large warehouse stores away from the centre. Late-night shopping until as late as 8pm is on Thursday in Oxford and Regent streets and on Wednesday in Knightsbridge and Kensington.

Postal Services

Post Offices are open Monday to Friday 9am–5pm, Saturday 9am–noon. Stamps are available from post offices and selected shops, usually newsagents, and from machines outside most post offices. Within the UK sending a letter first class costs 25 pence and second class, which is slower, costs 19 pence. These are increased by weight.

London's main post office is at Trafalgar Square, situated on the east side behind the church of St Martin-in-the-Fields. It stays open until 8pm Monday to Saturday. Beware, queues tend to be long over the lunch period.

Post-haste

Public telephones

There are five different types of public phone boxes. The oldest type requires users to insert 10p coins after dialling but before speaking. Making long-distance calls will require many 10p coins which have to be inserted during the call. For the more modern type of phone box, coins are inserted before dialling, but not all coins are accepted. Another type uses credit cards and another type uses Phonecards (They are easily distinguished by the word 'Phonecard' on a green panel). These convenient cards can be purchased from post offices and shops and are available in units of 40, 100 or 200. The card is pushed into the slot and the units used are automatically erased.

In 1994 the dialling codes for London were changed. **0171** is for the inner London area and **0181** is for the outer ring. The codes should be used even when phoning from within Greater London.

Directory Enquiries within the UK, tel: **192**.

International calls: You can telephone abroad directly by dialling 010 followed by the country code and then the number. Codes can be obtained from the International Operator by dialling 155. Dial 155 to make a collect call (reverse charge) or to make a charge to your credit card at home. You will be charged extra for operator-assisted calls. International Directory Enquiries is 154. To send telegrams, dial 193.

Sprint, tel: 0800 89 0877; AT&T, tel: 0800 89 0011; MCI, tel: 0800 89 0222.

Emergency numbers: police, ambulance or fire brigade, tel: **999**.

Service charges and tips

Most hotels and many restaurants automatically add 10–15 percent service charge to your bill. It's your right to deduct it if you're not happy with the service. Sometimes when service has been added, the final total on a credit card slip will still be left blank the implication being that a further tip is expected. In London, you don't tip in pubs, cinemas, theatres or elevators. You do tip hairdressers, sightseeing guides, railway porters and cab drivers. They get around 10 percent. Cab drivers will expect 15 percent on smaller fares.

A Savoy start to the day

Accommodation

Hotel accommodation in London is expensive. The British Tourist Authority (*see page 98*) recommends a booklet entitled *Where to Stay in London*. The accommodation listed in another BTA publication called *London Budget Hotels* is good value.

Accommodation service

The British Travel Centre (12 Regent Street, south of Piccadilly Circus) and the information desks run by the LTB at Victoria Station, Liverpool Street Station, Selfridges department store and Heathrow Airport, Terminals 1, 2 and 3 Underground concourse (*see page 98*) run an accommodation service and will find rooms in hotels and guest houses, charging only a small fee. Accommodation can also be booked on tel: 0171-824 8844; have your Visa, Access or MasterCard details ready.

Hotels

Luxury hotels (**££££**) offer the very best accommodation, category 1 (**£££**) hotels are described as first-class, category 2 (**££**) are good family hotels and category 3 (**£**) are less expensive hotels.

The following hotels are in central London and the prices shown are the minimum prices for one person in a double room with breakfast: **££££** from £100, **£££** from £50, **££** from £30 and **£** from £20–£30.

Some suggested hotels:
££££ Athenaeum, 116 Piccadilly, W1V 0BJ; **Grosvenor House**, Park Lane, W1A 2HH; **Hyde Park**, Knightsbridge, SW1Y 7LA; **Le Meridien London**, 21 Piccadilly, W1V 0BH; **The Savoy**, The Strand, WC2R 0EU.

1 At your service

£££ Coburg Hotel, Bayswater Rd, W2 4RJ; **Cumberland**, Marble Arch, W1A 4RF; **Ramada**, Berners Street, W1A 3BE; **Stakis St Ermin's**, Craxton Street, SW1H 0QW; **Tower Thistle**, St Katharine's Way, E1 9LD; **Waldorf**, Aldwych, WC2B 4DD.

££ Eden Plaza, 68 Queen's Gate, SW7 5JT; **Kingsley Hotel**, Bloomsbury Way, WC1A 2SD; **Montana Hotel**, 67 Gloucester Rd, SW7 4PG; **Richmond Gate Hotel**, Richmond Hill, TW10 6RP; **Royal Norfolk Hotel**, 25 London Street, W2 1HH.

£ Atlas Hotel, 24–30 Lexham Gardens, W8 5JE; **Lexham Hotel**, 32–38 Lexham Gardens, W8 5JE; **McCready Hotel**, 357–363 Romford Road, Forest Gate, E7 8AA; **Parkside Hotel**, 384 Seven Sisters Road, Finsbury Park, N4 2PQ; **Rhodes House Hotel**, 195 Sussex Gardens, W2 2RJ; **Windermere Hotel**, 42 Warwick Way, SW1V 4EJ.

At your service

Bed and breakfast

Private rooms are usually very clean and good value, cooking facilities are often provided. The magazine *London Weekly Advertiser* is a good place to find details. B&B hotels have signs by their gate or in the window.

103

Youth Hostels, YMCA, YWCA

City Hostel, 36 Carter Lane, EC4 5AD, tel: 0171-236 4965 (*nearest Underground station: St Paul's/Blackfriars*); **Earl's Court**, 38 Bolton Gardens, SW5 0AQ, tel: 0171- 373 7083 (*nearest Underground station: Earl's Court*); **Hampstead Heath**, 4 Wellgarth Road, NW22 7HR, tel: 0181-458 9054 (*nearest Underground station: Golders Green*); **Highgate Village**, 84 Highgate West Hill, N6 6LU, tel: 0181-340 1831 (*nearest Underground station: Archway/Highgate*); **Holland House**, Holland Walk, W8 7QU, tel: 0171-937 0748 (*nearest Underground station: Holland Park/High Street Kensington*); **Oxford Street**, 14 Noel Street, W1V 3PD, tel: 0171-734 1618 (*nearest Underground station: Oxford Circus/Tottenham Court Road*); **Rotherhithe**, Salter Road, SE16 1LY, tel: 0171-232 2144 (*nearest Underground: Rotherhithe*).

YMCA/YWCA: A full list of YMCA hostels can be obtained from the National Council of YMCAs, 640 Forest Road, Walthamstow, E17 3DZ.

Student accommodation

Between July and September, rooms in some student hostels and halls of residence at universities can be rented by tourists and holiday-makers. Contact: BUAC, Box No. 391, University Park, Nottingham, N7 2RD.

Index